T4-ADF-721

THE EXPULSION OF THE JEWS AND THEIR EMIGRATION TO THE SOUTHERN LOW COUNTRIES
(15th-16th c.)

ML

MEDIAEVALIA LOVANIENSIA

Editorial Board

C. Steel
J. Goossens
G. Latré
W. Verbeke

SERIES I / STUDIA XXVI

KATHOLIEKE UNIVERSITEIT LEUVEN
INSTITUUT VOOR MIDDELEEUWSE STUDIES
LEUVEN (BELGIUM)

THE EXPULSION OF THE JEWS AND THEIR EMIGRATION TO THE SOUTHERN LOW COUNTRIES
(15th-16th C.)

Edited by

Luc DEQUEKER
and
Werner VERBEKE

LEUVEN UNIVERSITY PRESS
1998

© 1998 by Leuven University Press/Presses Universitaires de Louvain/
Universitaire Pers Leuven, Blijde-Inkomststraat 5
B-3000 Leuven/Louvain (Belgium)

*All rights reserved, including the right to translate or
to reproduce this book or parts thereof in any form*

ISBN 90 6186 864 5
D/1998/1869/6

CONTENTS

Preface   VII

Julien KLENER, *Introduction: Spanish Jewry at the Eve of the Expulsion*   IX

Eleazar GUTWIRTH, *Jewish and Christian Messianism in XVth Century Spain*   1

Hyam MACCOBY, *The Tortosa Disputation, 1413-14, and its Effects*   23

Enrique GONZÁLEZ GONZÁLEZ, *Vives: Un humanista judeoconverso en el exilio de Flandes*   35

George HUGO TUCKER, *To Louvain and Antwerp, and Beyond: The contrasting itineries of Diogo Pires (Didacus Pyrrhus Lusitanus, 1517-99) and João Rodrigues de Castelo Branco (Amatus Lusitanus, 1511-68)*   83

Index   115

PREFACE

The present volume originates from a colloquium which was organized by the Belgian *Institutum Judaicum* and the *Instituut voor Middeleeuwse Studies* of the *Katholieke Universiteit Leuven* in a common effort to commemorate the tragical events in the history of European Jewry around 1492. The organisers intended to elucidate neglected aspects of the spiritual landscape of medieval Spain on the eve of the expulsion and to draw the attention, by way of a few examples, to the sequels of Jewish emigration for the intellectual circles in the Southern Low Countries during the 16th century.

The editors would like to express their gratitude to all who, in one way or another, have contributed to the colloquium and the realisation of this volume in the *Mediaevalia Lovaniensia*.

Special thanks are also due, for various kinds of financial as well as moral support, to the *Fonds voor Wetenschappelijk Onderzoek-Vlaanderen*, to the *Arts Faculty* of the *Katholieke Universiteit Leuven* and to the *Institutum Judaicum*.

JULIEN KLENER

INTRODUCTION :
SPANISH JEWRY AT THE EVE OF THE EXPULSION

In the last decades preceding the expulsion, Jewish life in Spain was in many aspects completely different from the living circumstances existing during the so-called Golden age between the 10th and the 13th century. The clear break with earlier times is often chronologically situated in the tragic year of 1391, but the events marking the end of the fourteenth century where themselves the result of a general atmosphere and a political situation created by the christian kings of Spain -Castile, Aragon and Navarre - since about a century.

It seems therefore worthwhile, before sketching the actual situation preceding the expulsion, to rerun the history of the earlier period.

It is overwell known that the Fourth Lateran Council of 1215 called by pope Innocent III with it's overtly anti-Jewish decrees and the creation of mendicant friars, marks the definite break-down of the Jewish social status in the whole of Western-Europe[1]. In a letter addressed to the count of Nevers, Innocent III summed up his policy: "The Jews like the fratricide Cain, are doomed to wander about the earth as fugitives and vagabonds, and their faces must be covered in shame. They are under no circumstances to be protected by Christian princes, but, on the contrary, condemned to serfdom"[2]. Nevertheless these measures had no immediate impact on the Spanish kings. The permanent wars against the Moors continued, and step by step the peninsula was reclaimed for the cross. But the small kingdoms that emerged with each Christian victory showed little animosity towards their Jewish inhabitants, most probably because the kings needed everyone in order to fulfill their dream of reconquista and in so doing could not permit any inner strive.

Unfortunately these halcyon days were soon interrupted and then ended. In the middle of the 13th century war with islam was almost

---

1. Amongst other things Jews had to wear a special sort of dress in order to distinguish them from the Christians. St. Louis of France, before departing for a new crusade against the Turks, insisted upon a badge of red or saffron-yellow in form of a wheel, to be worn on back and breast both "so that those who were thus marked might be recognized from all sides". See S. SCHWARZFUCHS, *Les Juifs de France,* Paris, 1975, p. 85.
2. A.L. SACHAR, A *History of the Jews,* New York, 1965, p. 193.

over, and the pressure of the church on society was becoming overstrong.

In fact, the middle of the 13th century, especially the reign of the Castilian king Alfonso X (1252-1284) contains the basic aspects and, with historical hindsight, the premonitory signs of the decline of Spanish Jewry. During his reign Alfonso X sought to limit the force of the special privileges of individuals and municipalities, which formed until that time the basis of the juridical system in Castile, and to replace them with a "national system of law, uniformly binding upon all elements of the population"[3]. This attitude might be considered as the beginning of a centralized form of government, which in the 15th and 16th century, would lead to the search of a complete identity between society and the functioning within that same society of a specific faith. An approach which Luther would later describe as the principle of identity between "regio et religio"[4].

Furthermore during the same period the famous code of law associated with the name of Alfonso X, *Las Siete Partidas*, confirms the Church legislation concerning the Jews and from under the dust of history this code actual ly links up with the ancient Visigothic discriminatory attitude.

True, the code did not go into effect until the middle of the fourteenth century but it does, however, reflect changing ideological currents concerning the Jews.

Another changing factor is the growing power of the mendicant friars[5] leading amongst other fateful signs for the future of the Jews to the disputation which was held in Barcelona in 1263 in the presence of the king, the bishop and leading Aragonese Dominicans, like Raymond Martini, the author of the infamous *Pugio Fidei* "The Dagger of Faith"[6], the most important and widely circulated medieval anti-Jewish

---

3. Y. BEAR, A *History of Jews in Christian Spain 1* (HJCS), Philadelphia, 1978, p. 115.

4. See L.S. FERNANDEZ, "*La population juive à la veille de 1492. Causes et mécanismes de l'expulsion*", pp. 39-41, in H. MECHOULAN, *Les Juifs d'Espagne: histoire d'une diaspora 1492-1942,* Paris, 1992.

5. J. COHEN, *The Friars and the Jews, The Evolution of Medieval Anti-Judaism,* Ithaca-London, 1982, passim.

6. See H. JANSEN, *Raymond Martini's manuscript Pugio Fidei infecteert West en Oost,* Kampen, 1990. The fact that R. Martini published his *Pugio Fidei* in 1278 might indicate that the christian arguments used during the disputation of Barcelona needed rethinking and reworking.

polemic, supplying dubious source material to disputant friars and Jewish apostates. In 1263 the chief propagandist against his former faith was the apostate Pablo Christiani, standing model for later overzealous apostates, like Solomon Halevi, the rabbi of Burgos, and Joshua ibn Vives Halorqi. Both converted, probably for ideological reasons and were known in their new faith as Paulus de Sancta Maria and Hieronymus de Sancta Fide[7]. In the same period we also notice the first interferences of the Inquisition in Jewish affairs, with the dispute raging around Maimonides's books and the possible burning of parts of his books by the Dominicans in 1233, probably at the request of Salomon ben Abraham from Montpellier[8].

Nevertheless the middle of the 13th century is still a transitional time. King Alfonso X the Wise, himself a scholar and a patron of learning, extended to Jewish scholars a hospitality not found in the courts of any of his contemporaries, f.i. rabbi Isaac ibn Cid, the cantor of the Toledo synagogue and Rabbi Judah ben Moses ha-Kohen participated in the preparation of the famous Alphonsine (planetary) Tables[9].

The first very concrete signs of the deterioration became visible when Navarre fell to France in 1285 and its Jews were soon subjected to the restrictions and degradations endured by their co-religionists on the other side of the Pyrenees. The French example was sufficiently impressed upon Navarre and by 1328 there were massacres or matanzanes[10] in Estella, Tudela and other large centers, in which over six thousand Jews lost their lives.

Clerical agitators, religious disputations and trials before the papal inquisition, helped to bring Aragon into line with Navarre and soon even the statute-books reflected the general animosity of the masses, creating an atmosphere of agression against the Jews, which led in the first place to their losing the possibility of occupying public office.

In the kingdom of Castile things changed more slowly and Jews could still attain high esteemed social positions during the 14th century as was the case with Don Yuçaf of Ecija at the service of Alfonso XI (1322-1350)[11], with Don Samuel ben Meir Abulafia king Pedro the

---

7. They played pivotal roles in later disputations. Cfr. note 13.
8. See HJCS 1, p. 108-110; see also B. MARTIN, A *History of Judaism*, II, New York, 1979, p. 74.
9. HJCS 1, p. 120.
10. B. LEROY, *The Jews of Navarra*, Jerusalem, 1985, p. 17.
11. He was appointed almoxarife mayor, organizing the administration of taxes and other finance for the entire kingdom. See A. BALLESTEROS, *Don Yuçaf de Ecya*, in *Sefarad* VI (1946), pp. 253-287.

Cruel's financier and chief treasurer, who helped build the beautiful El Transito-synagoge in Toledo, which still stands to this day or with Meir Alguadez, the personal doctor of John I at the end of the 14th century. But although in the beginning of the 14th century Castile remained fairly faithful to its tradition of tolerance, it turned too. The animosity of the masses being already influenced by remaining rumours surrounding the Black Death epidemic, lead to the effective downfall of Jews starting during the virulent Castilian civil war (1366-1369) between king Pedro the Cruel (1350-1369) and his bastard brother Henry of Trastamara[12]. Henry using willfully the existing anti-Jewish feelings within the population, stated that Pedro, and with him the whole country was in their hands, and that he would liberate Castile from their grip. After his victory Henry tempered his dislike of Jews, but things had gone to far and togetherness between Christians and Jews had passed a turning-point and were thenceforth completely jeopardised. At the same time the Jewish community suffered a deep spiritual crisis. Many Jews, especially the influential ones had lost their faith[13], a fact underlined in the work *Seda(h) la-Derek* by Menahem ibn Zerah (1310-1385), who writes reprovingly of those Jews who because of the demands of the times disregard the observance of the precepts. To have a further idea of the spiritual decline one has to compare the almost non-existing consequences of the earlier mentioned July 1263-disputation at the court of Aragon during the reign of James I, with Nahmanides leading the Jewish party, with the consequences of the disputation of Tortosa[14] held in 1413-1414, tending to many voluntary conversions[15].

The general climate of hostility towards the Jews at the end of the 14th century was so intense that a spark could ignite an explosion. The actual detonator being the violent sermons against the Jews launched by Ferrant Martinez, the archdeacon of Ecija, demanding conversion through all means. On the first of Tammuz 5151 (June 4, 1391) riots

---

12. See J. VALDERÓN BARUQUE, *Los Judíos de Castilla y la revolución trastamara*, Valladolid, 1968.

13. Parts of Spanish Jewry were also influenced by the Averoist philosophy and the clash between reason and faith.

14. The prosecuting counsel was the convert Joshua ibn Vives Halorqi, the papal physician, functioning under his new name Hieronymus de Sancta Fide.

15. Amongst them several members of the influential Cavalleria family from Saragossa.

breaking out in Seville led to the butchering of several thousand Jews; other thousands were driven into baptism to escape death and hundreds were sold as slaves to the Moors.

The riots spread throughout Spain for the following three months. Cordoba, Toledo, Madrid, Valencia, Palma de Mallorca, Gerona, Logroño, Burgos witnessed the devastation of Jewish quarters with thousands of lives snuffed out and tens of thousands of forced baptisms[16].

The fury of 1391 had three main consequences on Jewish life during the ultimate phase of their presence in Spain:
- the decline or the disappearance of the large Jewish communities;
- the dispersion of the remaining Jews throughout the Spanish countryside and
- the presence of a very large number of converts.

Following the 1391-events some of the most important Jewish communities, Barcelona and Valencia, disappeared completely. Others like Toledo, Seville, Burgos were depopulated and lost their importance. There would never again be Jewish centres like Toledo, Barcelona or Burgos, real beacons of social and intellectual life[17].

In 1391 the larger the community, the more they suffered. This brought the remaining Jews to leave the main cities and settle in numerous small towns and villages, even in places where Jews had never resided. Most probably the idea was that distance from the important agglomerations could mean distance from political turmoil. Seventy to eighty years later some communities again counted 1500 people (less than half the erstwhile population of Valencia, Barcelona or Toledo), but a large Jewish community would mean 500 people and the average Jewish presence in one place was lower than 100 souls. Furthermore, the larger communities were situated in cities like Ocaña and Maqueda, near Toledo, Trujillo in Extremaduro, or Zamora, Almazan and Amusco in northern Castile, places that had no influence on the political, economical and cultural life of the kingdom. This of course meant for Jews a more quiet and saver life, but also less impact on the king's court[18].

---

16. See C.C. PARRONDO, *Le Judaïsme espagnol avant l'exil,* in H. MECHOULAN, *op.cit.,* pp. 21-28.

17. J.L. LACAVE, *La société juive et l'aljama à l'époque de l'expulsion,* in H. Mechoulan, *op.cit.,* p. 13.

18. J.L. LACAVE, *op.cit.,* p. 4.

The third phenomenon was of course the vast group of converts, which were going to be one of the crucial problems of Spanish society in the 15th century and indirectly one of the main causes of the expulsion of 1492.

To the many Jews baptized in 1391 in order to save their life, were added in the thirty following years a steady stream of converts. The pressure of the Church, the general atmosphere together with the apparent facility with which the converts were accepted into the Christian society, convinced many more to be baptized. Campaigns lead by the Dominican preacher Vicente Ferrer or the above mentioned disputation of Tortosa organised by Cardinal Pedro de Luna (later antipope Benedict XIII) attracted many more Jews, so that by 1415 their number was that vast that they formed an own group within Christian society.

Otherwise from the year 1415 on, those remaining faithful to Judaism tried to reconstruct their Jewish life. Sudden changes in the Catholic church and the royal courts of Spain[19] saved the Jews at a moment when they seemed on the verge of destruction and they took the possibility to build up their communal life again. Later on we will mention a famous rabbinical meeting in Valladolid in 1432[20]. Anyhow the wholesale conversions created a problem, which would weigh heavily on the Jews. In fact, the Christian society of the 15th century became divided into two factions, the old Christians and the new. The Church and the Crown, intended to mold the new Christians into good Christians, started to hinder Jewish life. This was especially clear with the reformatory laws concerning Jews promulgated on the 2nd of January 1412 by the government of Castile. The frames of the law obviously intented to degrade the Jews to the status of "hewers of wood and drawers of water" for the Christians[21].

Inevitably a wedge of misunderstanding cut through the relations of the old and new Christians. Since the twelfth century, popular superstition based on theological approaches had presented Jews as a social and physical danger. But at least Jews, as such, were an "open and public" danger; they were known, they lived in recognizable communities, they were forced to bear distinguishing marks and dress. But when

---

19. In Castile, John II (1406-1454) and in Aragon, Alfonso V (1416-1458) took over the throne. Both were more interested in secular culture than in religious fanaticism, and showed willingness to restore the Jewish communities of their countries.

20. See p. XVII.

21. HJCS 2, pp. 167-168.

they became converts, they became a hidden danger. Spanish townsfolk knew that many, perhaps most, of the conversos were reluctant and had ceased formally to be Jews from fear, or to gain advantage. As Jews they suffered from severe legal disabilities. As conversos they had the same economic rights, in theory, as other Christians. A converso was thus much more unpopular than a practising Jew because he was an interloper in trade and craft, an economic threat; and since he was probably a secret Jew, he was a hypocrite and a hidden subversive too. Furthermore converts were despised for their success in winning important state positions and penetrating into the sanctum sanctorum of the church. They were also rejected for what was seen by many as a cynical adherence to Catholic practices.

How deep the animosity against the new Christians had become was demonstrated in 1449 when Toledo became the scene of an assault on their houses. All the new Christians who attempted to defend themselves or their property were beaten or killed[22]. The king's attempts to restore order failed and he was compelled to watch as the council passed on edict forbidding new Christians to hold any public office. This revolt was definitely religious in character but with the extra dimension that "once a Jew, always a Jew". This approach might be linked to an emerging vision concerning the existence of different human races that lead in the following century to fundamental discussions concerning the soul of the American Indians. In fact the events happening in Toledo in 1449 could be seen as genuine race-hatred[23].

And so between 1478 and 1481 the Spanish Inquisition, which would deal the death-blow to Spanish Jewry, started it's activities[24]. The institution was originally directed against the judaizing converts, but very soon the inquisitors realized that they would never eradicate the judaïzers as long as actual Jews could freely practice their religion. The influence of the inquisitors was decisive upon the decision by Catholic kings to expulse the Jews[25]. The decree signed on March 31st 1492 and made public one month later ordered all Jews, on pain of

22. HJCS II, p. 279.
23. A.A. SICROFF, *Les Controverses des Statuts de pureté de Sang en Espagne du XVe au XVIe siècle,* Paris, 1960, passim.
24. See f.i. L. POLIAKOV, *De Mahomet aux Marranes,* Paris, 1961, pp. 170-201.
25. See M. KRIEGEL, *Les Juifs à la fin du Moyen Age dans l'Europe méditerrannéenne,* Paris, 1979. H. BEINART, *Trials of the Spanish Inquisition in Cuidad Réal,* 4 vol., Jerusalem, 1974-1985.

death, to leave the country within three months. In 1498 Jews also had to leave the kingdom of Navarre and with this last expulsion no more Jews were officially present on the Iberian peninsula.

After this brief resketching of the historical frame work we may now try an even more succint analysis of life and social situation of the Jews in the last decades preceding the expulsion. As said earlier, life was different compared to before 1391, but still some common traits were preserved. The main difference being of course the disappearance of glorious Jewish communities like Toledo and Barcelona, the Jewish presence in smaller less important agglomerations and the conversos.

In this last period of the Jewish history in Spain the major part of the Jewish population were artisans, had small businesses or lived from moneylending. The Jews supported themselves mostly dealing in textile, furs, fabric and also jewelry. Tannery also appears as a typical Jewish activity in many cities. In the documents we further encounter potters and ceramists, shoemakers, dyers, silver- and goldsmiths, masons and joiners. But some trades which were considered as typical Jewish like chemist or spicehandler would completely disappear due to the many interdictions[26].

The number of Jewish moneylenders mentioned in the documents of the 2nd part of the 15th century seems much higher than in previous centuries, most probably this had to do with the prohibition for the Jews to exercise a number of other professions. Moneylending was sharply condemned by the Church and often it attempted to abolish or diminish the moneylending activities, but reality always prevailed. Credit was necessary for a number of activities, especially in agriculture. On the other hand the nobility and the kings were inclined to protect Jewish moneylending, afraid of being deprived of the taxes they imposed on the Jews[27].

In any way moneylending was a risky trade because it was difficult to collect the interests, therefore Jewish moneylenders often had another occupation too. In the financial administration of Castile the practice of farming state revenues to individuals remained in place. The revenue farmers were for the most part Jews. In the 15th century a whole network of Jewish tax-farmers was spread over the entire kingdom. Their chief was a Jewish tax-farmer general who also acted as the

---

26. J.L. LACAVE, *op. cit.*, pp. 13-14.
27. See J.L. LACAVE, *op.cit.*, pp. 14-15; See B. LEROY, *op.cit.*, pp. 98 sq.

king's treasurer. This post was held during the reign of John II[28] by Don Abraham Bienveniste of Soria. The tax-farmer general was an important personality at the king's court. During the reign of the so-called Catholic Kings the office was held by Abraham Seneor[29] and his son-in-law rabbi Meir Melamed, who both converted to Christianity in July 1492.

Medicine also remained a typical Jewish profession. In almost all Jewish communities there was a doctor and in many cities Jewish doctors received an extra financial aid to cure also the rest of the population. Jews as personal physician of nobles, clergy and at the royal court were a classic phenomenon.

In many small places Jews owned property especially vineyards and gardens, fields and even pasture lands most of the time enough to assure kosher food[30]. That is why the butcher belonged to the central institutions of the aljama or independent Jewish community.

These aljama's possessed a wide field for independent inner political activity and functioned as a virtual autonimous body. They were charged with the regulations of religious, social, juridical and economic life of its members. In the 15th century after the pogroms of 1391, the oppressive legislation of 1412 and the devastating consequences of the Tortosa disputations a more centralized structure seemed necessary. This internal reform was initiated by Don Abraham Bienveniste, court-rabbi (Rab de la Corte)[31] of Castile by government appointment. In 1432 he convoked delegates of the remaining aljama's in Valladolid, where they convened in the great synagogue. The assembly issued five unique sets of regulations aimed to restore the life of the communities and so promoted an internal revival. As the meeting was held in the chief city, the seat of the chief rabbi, it also expressed the idea of a Castilian national Jewish organization. The statutes were written with Hebrew letters in a mixture of Hebrew and Castilian. Out of these takkanot, we learn that to be recognized as an aljama the local community had to possess all official institutions prescribed by the rab-

28. HJCS 2, p. 250. See also note 30.
29. E. GUTWIRTH, *Abraham Senior: Social Tensions and the Court-Jew*, in *Michaël* 11 (1989), pp. 169-229.
30. H. BEINART, *La Société Hispano-Juive*, in *Génie du Judaïsme*, Paris, 1975, p.213.
31. Also to be considered as chief rabbi. See Rab de la Corte, EJ 13, col. 1468-1469.

binical legislation: a house of worship, a ritual bath, a butcher and a organized public instruction. Every Jewish family had to collect indirect taxes on meat, wine, weddings, circumcision and death. Some of this money had to be used in order to engage a good children's teacher in every community of fifteen families. In communities of 40 families a teacher of Torah had to be maintained. The aljama had the right to draw up statutes of its own which had to be approved publicly in synagogue[32], and later sanctioned through royal approval[33].

Normally the governing board of the aljama was elected yearly[34]. The most important function in Aragon, as well as in Castile was the adelantado (mukadamin), which represented the executive power. The dayanim, the communal judges always operating by three, represented the judicial power. They had to be chosen in each community "to consider claims, grievances and complaints, and punish trangressions"[35]. Especially heavy were the sentences for informers (malsinut), and denouncing Jews to Christians. Theoretically even the death-penalty was possible, as wel as excommunication[36].

Nevertheless it is unclear wether the aljama's even enforced these laws in the course of the last decades before the expulsion. Changing political view being the complete identity between society and the faith professed by that same society had been reached. On the one hand the rulers of Spain could not ignore that their kingdom had become an exception as, elsewhere in the West, judaism had almost disappeared (England, 18th July 1290; Brabant, May or June 1370; France 1394). Furthermore the Catholic church insisted since ages on the dangers of coexistence between Christians and Jews. So it is not only the presence of the Conversos, with their terrible identity-problems, which lead to the expulsion. The stereotypes for distancing the Jews lived since long in Christian societies. And even if the decree of expulsion was drafted by Tomas de Torquemada, and thus the work of the Holy Office, the general atmosphere concerning Jews can be formulated as follows: "Au mieux, les infidèles pouvaient accéder a un statut de simple tolérance,

---

32. See Y.M. KOCH, *The Takanoth of Valladolid of* 1432, in *The American Sephardi,* 9 (1978), pp. 58-145.
33. *Ibid.*
34. HJCS II, p. 262.
35. *Ibid.* See H. BEINART, *La Société etc...,* p. 223.
36. HJCS II, 5.

mais faut-il rappeler que l'on ne tolère que tout ce que l'on a réprouvé, et qu'en fait on souhaite sa disparition"[37].

Apart from the religious motives it may not be forgotten that Ferdinand and Isabella had also reasons of state, being strong advocates of an identification between the religious and the political structures within a state. They had established to reach that goal the National Spanish Inquisition in 1478. When then the Holy Office wanted the expulsion of Jews, the Catholic kings could and would nothing else but agree seeing it as their duty to state and church.

Both Ferdinand and Isabella claimed that they were indeed acting purely from orthodox and Catholic zeal. Both hotly rejected the charge made by their enemies at the time and by some historians since, that they wanted to confiscate the property of convicted heretics[38]. The truth seems to be that both monarchs were driven by a mixture of religious and financial motives, and also importantly, by the desire to impose a centralizing, emotional unity on their disparate and divided territories. But most of all they were caught up in the sinister impersonal logic of anti-judaism itself.

They signed the decree and the destruction of Spanish Jewry was a fact. It also was the most momentous event in Jewish history since the mid-second century. Now a large and gifted community was dispersed all over the Mediterranean and Moslem world, and from Portugal, in a later Sephardi diaspora, to France and north-west Europe. What Spain lost others gained and in the long run the Sephardi diaspora was to prove exceedingly creative and of critical importance in Jewish development and in consolidating the wonderfully Jewish perrenity.

---

37. L.S. FERNANDEZ, *La population juive à la veille de 1492. Causes mécanismes de l'expulsion*, in MESHULAN, *op.cit.*, p. 40.

38. See L.S. FERNANDEZ, *op.cit.*, pp. 39-40. H. KAMEN, *The Mediterrannean and the Expulsion of Spanish Jews in 1492*, in *Past and Present*, 119 (1988), pp. 30-55.

Eleazar GUTWIRTH

JEWISH AND CHRISTIAN MESSIANISM IN XVth CENTURY SPAIN

I

The author of the *Quixote* wrote a play in verse while he was in captivity in Argel in the 1570's: *La gran sultana doña Catalina de Oviedo.* In it, he wanted to underline every religion's perseverance in maintaining its faith. Cervantes wishes to represent the type of insult that could be leveled at a Jew by a Christian. The Christian character's invective is: 'vanquished people/ infamous, dirty race'/'gente aniquilada/ infame, sucia raza'. The reason for Jewish decline is: 'your vain waiting, your madness/ your incomparable stubbornness' 'vuestro vano esperar, vuestra locura/ y vuestra incomparable pertinacia.'[1]

This representation of the Jew as a messianic being, as 'the one who waits' is well known to students of Golden Age Spanish literature. But it is relevant to our theme. It may be suggested that it is part of a much older tradition of anti-Jewish invective in Spanish Christian literature. In the *Trivagia,* towards the end of Juan del Encina's poem, we find the following lines: 'And you Rabbi of false countenance/ you fool yourself by falsifying your prophecies/ hoping still for the coming of the Messiah/ although he has already come and he was even of your lineage...' "Y tu Rabbi de falso visaje/ te enganas falsando las tus prophecias/ que esperas que aun deva venir el Messias/ aviendo venido, y aun de tu linaje..."[2] The messianic topos may easily be traced back to the fifteenth century. Antón de Montoro wrote a satiric poem of invective against a fellow *converso*, Ruy or Rodrigo Cota. Amongst other allusions to Cota's Jewish ancestry and character, there are the following lines: 'And you lord of valour, / wisdom and good brains/ as there are no Messiahs left/ let go of knighthood/ and take on the measuring rod and the scales' "Y vos senor de valias/ de sauer y de buen seso/ pues que no quedan mexias/ dexad las cauallerias/ y tomad la vara y peso".[3] The sense of the invective is clear: Montoro advises Cota to renounce

---

1. A. Castro, *Cervantes y los casticismos españoles* (Madrid, 1974), p. 77.
2. Juan del Encina, *Obras Completas*, II, ed. A.M. Rambaldo (Madrid, 1978), p. 243.
3. *Cancionero,* ed. C. Carrete (Madrid, 1984), p. 357.

the attempts at being a Spanish Christian and return to his Judaism. The allusion to *cauallerias* is metonymic of the whole Christian Spanish *persona* and so is the measuring rod, typical of the Jew involved in textiles in general and clothing in particular. Equally charged with malicious meaning is the *peso*, the weighting measure of the Jewish merchant at the market. The key antithesis would seem to be contained in the rhyme *mexias / cauallerias* where belief in the Messiah is as emblematic of being a Jew as chivalry stands for the new class he aspires to in Christian society. Such a selective view of Judaic belief and practice is by no means restricted to the literary genres mentioned above. It was part of the general Christian Spanish view of the Jews, preserved for us not only in drama and poetry, but also in other genres, such as theological treatises of polemics. A purely random example, out of many that could be adduced, is the recently rediscovered work of Diego Ramírez de Villaescusa, founder of the Colegio de Santiago el Zebedeo, *De religione christiana...* dedicated to the Catholic Monarchs between 1500-1504. Its fourth Treatise attempts to argue "ex auctoritatibus a iudaeis receptis christum in lege et prophetis promissum iam venisse".[4] Montoro's, Encina's, Cervantes' and the many other instances of such invective depend on the perception of the Jew's Messianism as an 'essential' part of his character or faith. Modern historians or critics who take for granted a general Jewish Messianism, central to the faith and therefore, unchanged by geographic or historic context, might be said to be adopting these old topoi we have documented. On the other hand, long term ideas cannot be dismissed completely. On the contrary, internal, Hebrew sources may show the precise forms in which such beliefs were articulated in fifteenth century Spain. One clearly defined genre is that of homiletics. Shem Tov ben Joseph ben Shem Tov finished his book of homilies in 1489, shortly before the Expulsion. If we take the conclusion of his first homily on the Genesis pericope we read[5]: "let the day come which is all Sabbath. The day which is neither day nor night. As it says in the text with which we began. And that day is the Great Sabbath which is the world to come. And my beloved will come into his garden. And he shall eat the fruit of his delight. And the evildoer shall be banned from it... and the just shall shine as the splendour of the heavens...". The conclusion

---

4. F. Marcos Rodríguez, 'Un manuscrito perdido de Diego Ramírez Villaescusa', *RET* 20 (1960), 263-276.

5. *Derashot* (Salonika, 1525), f. 6 verso, col. a-b.

to the first wedding sermon in his homiletic collection reads [f. 7 verso col. a]: "let him not marry for beauty, and not in order to have children, who will help him at the gates, and not for wealth, but for the sake of heaven ...[then] he shall reach, and see the time when in the cities of Judea and in the outskirts of Jerusalem, shall be heard the voice of gladness and the sounds of joy... the voices of those who say: thank the Lord for he is good, for his lovingkindness is forever...". The allusion is to Jeremiah 33,11 where the prophet hopes for the restoration of Jerusalem: "Yet in this place shall be heard once again the sounds of joy and gladness, the voice of the bridegroom and the bride, here too shall be heard voices shouting, praised be the Lord of Hosts for he is good for his love endures forever". Again, at the conclusion of the sermon on the Noah pericope [f. 9 recto col. a] he concludes, aptly enough, with a quotation from that week's *haphtarah*: "may it be the will of the God of heaven that the time comes, the time of which it was said: 'for the waters of Noah'...". The allusion would be clear to his audience: the *haphtarah* they had just heard read out in Synagogue [Isaiah 54] begins: "Sing aloud! O barren woman, who never bore a child, now have I pitied you with a love which never fails, says the Lord... These days recall for me the days of Noah as I swore that the waters of Noah's flood should never again pour over the earth, so now I swear to you, never again to be angry with you or reproach you...". The message of the prophet was taken to have a clear messianic meaning. Most of the conclusions of the sermons in this Hispano-Jewish homiletic collection of 1489 have a similarly messianic ending. By the most basic rules of literary analysis, we must conclude that the messianic sensibility is 'purely formulaic'. Indeed the Sevilian liturgical codifier of the fourteenth century, David ben Joseph Abudarham, had spelled out (c. 1340) the custom, as it existed in his time and place: "it is customary to speak at the end of the sermon about verses [concerning] the redemption and holiness". The custom probably dates to at least the amoraic period.[6]

* *
*

---

6. *Sepher Abudarham* f. 45/4 (on W-ba le-Sion); See also L. Zunz, *Ha-drashot be-Israel* (Jerusalem, 1974), p. 174.

These two sets of Hispanic texts are not entirely random. The one shows the image of the Hispanic Jews in the perceptions of the Hispanic Christians. The other shows us a constant return to the theme of the Messiah or the messianic age in homiletic texts which are meant to represent the sermons delivered in the late fifteenth century Synagogues of Spain. In the climate of research of only a few years ago it would be unthinkable to take such texts into consideration when speaking of Jewish Messianism. Jewish Messianism was of interest only when it fulfilled certain conditions. The improvised terminology for describing these conditions as 'literary activism' 'propagandism' 'messianic speculation', is not necessarily the result of sustained theoretical thinking in the field of religious thought. It has been recently suggested that twentieth century political currents of thought determined the course of scholarship on Jewish Messianism.[7] The two sets of phenomena with which I began might lead us to question the criteria whereby only teleologically relevant aspects of Messianism are fit to be studied by the historian. Indeed, instead of using twentieth century ideology to set the priorities of research, one might try an alternative standard. That is to say, to see messianic ideas within their historical context. Such an attention to historical context would mean that one would no longer exclude attention to precise and up to date scholarship on the Hispanic Christian background of the precise period when Hebrew messianic texts were composed. It would also mean renouncing to see the literary evidence in isolation. On the contrary, a historical approach would concentrate on the links between the popular beliefs, as preserved in the archival documents in the various romance languages of the Iberian peninsula, for example, and the learned ideas in the written, Hebrew sources.

A further question which emerges is whether Jewish and Christian Messianism could possibly be commensurate with each other. Indeed, it has been suggested that there cannot be any resemblance between the spiritual Messianism of the Christians and the 'material' 'political' Messianism of the Jews:[8] "A *totally* different concept of redemption determines the attitude to Messianism in Judaism and Christianity... Judaism in *all* of its forms and manifestations has *always* maintained a concept of redemption which takes place publicly, on the stage of history and which *cannot be conceived* apart from such a visible appear-

---

7. M. Idel, 'Introduction' [Hebrew] to A.Z. Aescoly, *Jewish Messianic Movements,* Second Enlarged Edition (Jerusalem, 1987), p. 9/10.

8. G. Scholem, *The Messianic Idea in Judaism* (New York, 1971), p. 1.

ance. Christianity conceives of redemption as an event in the spiritual and unseen realm... [emphasis mine E.G.]".

The second problem, then is to reveal those areas of resemblance, and possibly coalescence, of Jewish and Christian Messianism. Here it is necessary to reveal my own bias: I am interested in Messianism as part of a project attempting to reconstruct the mind-set of fifteenth century Hispanic Jewry. My purpose here is not to try to explain Christian Spanish colonialist mentality in the post-expulsion period by discovering Jewish messianic 'influences'. Such a position could be found in the literature and it sees the ideas of Hispanic Jewry as relevant, only in so far as they can explain Christian-Spanish phenomena, rather than as valid historical issues in their own right, which should be studied in their original texts.

Thirdly, in addition to the problem of what is Messianism, and that of the validity of comparing Jewish and Christian manifestations, there is the problem of the periodization and of the geographical parameters. Indeed it is often maintained that the Messianism of post-expulsion texts although mostly associated with Jews of Hispanic origin, is a fundamentally post-expulsion phenomenon. It is a reaction to the crisis and trauma of Expulsion. Only recently has it been argued that there are messianic texts before the Expulsion, and that some of the messianic personalities associated with the post-1492 period had begun their activity before the Expulsion.

Finally, although there have been attempts at comparing both, Jewish and Christian messianic ideas, these have not conceded equal attention to both sides of the problem.

II

To test the hypothesis that totally different concepts of redemption determine the attitudes to Messianism in Judaism and Christianity, we might look at an example of a characteristic group of fifteenth century Spain: those *conversos* who were in touch with both Jewish and Christian texts. One such convert, who dealt with the messianic issue, is Maestre Juan el Viejo de Toledo. His work has been studied on the basis of the Madrid MS as representative of a type of *converso* mentality. The work is of importance, amongst other reasons, because it was transmitted in a medium – the Castilian romance – which was more likely to considerably influence contemporary thought than works of more restricted access written in Latin. Writers who are unaware of the state of lay literacy in fifteenth century Spain may not realize how marginal polemical works in Latin could be.[9] Here I should like to draw attention to one passage in his *Tratado* or *Memorial*. The passage belongs to the *Titulo Segundo* on "how the Messiah has already arrived". It comes after a number of sections in which various propositions are proved by passages from various prophets: e.g. 8b: "venga el profeta sacarias a dar fe como es ya venido" or f. 9b: "venga el profeta malachias a dar fe como es ya venido el mexias". The passage appears on folio xviii recto: "Of all the deadlines for the coming of the Messiah, which passed, one was by a scholar whose name was Rabbi Çag Abendino. He found the date which he said was true, and, according to his calculation, he had to come in the year of the robbery, which was the year 1390 [sic for 1391] of the birth of the saviour and he obtained this calculation by the letters in Hebrew. He had to come in the year 5151 from the Creation of the World. That was the year of the robbery of Jewry". This calculation can only be understood [lit. emmended= *emendar*] by someone who understands Hebrew. His calculation was as follows: he said "count what is the result of the sum of [the numerical value of] the letters of '*od hazon* which was said, by this prophet, Habakuk, who speaks of the Messiah, and the result of the sum of the [numerical value of the] Hebrew letters is a hundred and fifty one". They do not include the thousands, because there is no mistaking that computation. In that year, the Messiah came to us by force. And we were converted to the holy catholic faith. For on the day when a man comes to knowledge, on that day the Messiah comes to him. Thus it is said in the *Book of Çanhedrin*: Rabbi Joshua son of Levy asked Eliah: 'when shall the Messiah arrive? Eliah replied: Today. The day passed and he did not arrive. He said to him: what did you say? Eliah replied [he would come today] if you hearkened to his voice'. From this we understand that he who comes to knowledge, and hearkens to his voice, and believes in him, that same day the Messiah comes to him. And those of us who have converted to the holy catholic faith, the day on which we came and hearkened to his voice, that day the Messiah came. Thus I found, about the year of the robbery. All this chapter tries to prove the blindness of all those who hold that the Messsiah has not yet come and to prove how he has arrived and his coming was in the time of the Second House [Temple]."

---

9. Eleazar Gutwirth, 'Maestre Juan el Viejo and his Tratado (Madrid MS)', *Proceedings Ninth World Congress of Jewish Studies*, B (Jerusalem, 1986), 129-134: Biblioteca Nacional, Madrid, MS 9369.

This *converso* would, at first glance, seem to be discussing Messianism in terms which are totally foreign to the Jewish tradition. For him, the coming of the Messiah is an internal process of knowledge and faith: 'Hearkening', 'knowledge' and the private inner *'erlebniss'* of events, rather than visible alterations of cosmic and political order, are the key concepts in Maestre Juan el Viejo's text. But we now know that there is a Jewish tradition of 'spiritual' or 'inner' messianic interpretations and, moreover, we know that it was particularly richly articulated in the cultural area we are observing here, i.e. the Hispanic kingdoms. Examples may be found in Hispano-Jewish texts from the twelfth to the fifteenth centuries. These interpretations did not maintain a 'concept of redemption which takes place publicly', on the 'stage of history' and which cannot be conceived apart from such a visible appearance. Rather, they see redemption as an inner event. The interpretations vary: some maintain that it is the rejection of worldly desire; others write about the victory of the intelligibles over matter, or that of the 'forces of intellect and prophecy' over 'corporeality' and materialism.[10] This is a tradition according to which redemptive activity is the

10. M. Idel, 'Types of redemptive activity in the Middle Ages (Hebrew)', *Messianism and Eschatology,* ed. Z. Baras (Jerusalem, 1983), 253-280 (p. 254): Abraham b Hya in his *Meditations of the Sad Soul* (Hebrew) writes "... Man can acquire the world to come by an easy and small thing... to reject the desires of this world from the heart and the worldly desires and pleasures which are false and lying should be contemptible in your eyes... and by this act you shall cast off the yoke of this world from your neck and leave the exile and reach the heights of redemption and kingship". Man's initiative is that which brings about redemption. In the thirteenth century, Abulafia's *Sepher Ha-Melis* (Hebrew) provides a further example: "The growing horn which redeems the intellegibles from the kingdom of matter is man's intellect; it fights the material forces in man, vanquishes them and builds the Temple which is indestructible. The Temple is intellect. "Messianism is equated with intellectual labours. Most relevant is the *Toldot Adam* (Hebrew), a fifteenth century work. It develops the theme in a more clearly eschatological form: "... the separate intellect... is the comprehension of the divinity purified of all corporeality and from imaginary conceptions ... thus is death swallowed up forever and this aboliton is the great salvation which is the true salvation and the perfect redemption after which there is no exile. This [salvation] will be [brought about] by those two angels/ messengers the one is called Elijah and the second the son of David. I have already pointed out in previous chapters that Elijah is an allusion to the intellectual power but the son of David is an allusion to the prophetic powers for the son of David is named Solomon, the king with whom is peace [shalom] for he makes peace amongst all the forces. And the Jews shall dwell in peace in his days and he shall rule wisely over all men and he shall sit on the throne of the Lord and the form of a man will be above him and all the kings of the earth shall be subjected before him and bring him tribute... the power of prophecy is the son of David who will not prevail untill all the corporeal forces are consumed whose head is the imaginary and all the corporeal forces will be vanquished and hearken unto the intellect and prophecy".

ideal intellectual activity. That is to say, that in this aspect, Juan el Viejo's thought is not marginal to the tradition from which he emerged. On the contrary, he is firmly rooted in one strand of Jewish thinking about redemption. He may be emblematic of one area of contact between Jewish and Christian Messianism in fifteenth century Spain.

III

My second point has to do with the distinction between written and oral evidence. The impression of some students of Messianism as to the 'limpness' of pre-expulsion Messianism is generally the result of the study of written texts. Even these are, lately, yielding different results. But I should like to propose that we pay attention to *oral* utterances as well. Such a quest for the oral history of the Jewish Messianism of five hundred years ago would seem a 'methodological utopia' in most other fields of mediaeval Jewish studies. That it is possible in the study of xvth century Hispanic Jewry, is the result of the preservation of the files of Inquisition trials. Most of the studies on this type of documentation have been focused on the 'prophetic' aspects and on the *conversos*. But, it may be submitted, they are of interest to students of the non-converted Jews as well. This, not as a marginal appendage to the study of learned Hebrew texts, but as a major component of the phenomenon of the mentality of fifteenth century Hispanic Jewry.

Even if the messianic conclusions of the sermons the Jews heard in the Synagogues of Spain were 'formulaic', the messianic ideas articulated in them occupied their thought, and excited their interest, in real life even in the private sphere, before the Expulsion. They were subjects of conversations not only between the learned Kabbalists or theologians, whom we know from written treatises, but also between average Jewish individuals in the midst of their daily occupations. We may present some evidence from Inquisition records:[11] Jehuda Benardut was a tradesman from Calatayud who had commercial dealings with a former Jew, the *converso* Antón de Santangel. We have the records of a conversation they held around 1470, in the house of the converso, in what seems to be one of the better streets of the town. The space then, is private. Part of the conversation ran as follows: "You, Benardut, take

---

11. E. Marín Padilla, *Relación judeoconversa durante la segunda mitad del siglo XV en Aragón: La Ley* (Madrid, 1986), p. 140ff.

[from Christianity] that which is convenient; believe that he [Jesus] is the Messiah and not that he is God and man". Judah said "that is not well said: that would be a fourth religion". Antón, the converso, said: "I have only one religion, that is yours, the Jewish one which is a holy and a good religion. But I believe that the Messiah has come and you could believe this and thus come out of this captivity [i.e. the sufferings of being Jewish]". The theology is somewhat shaky, the ideas are by no means examples of the deepest achievements of either Jewish or Christian messianic thought. But, unlike the public pronouncements of preachers or Kabbalists, whether written or in sermon form, here we come much closer to placing socially the ideas on the Messiah. The evidence shows us these two businessmen who interrupt their commercial dealings and decide to speak about the Messiah. Talk about the Messiah was not the prerogative of men.[12] Gracia de Esplugas was a *conversa* of Saragossa who had converted around 1441/2. The few snippets of information we have about her show that she was neither a *beata* nor a dry theologian: testimonies in her Inquisition file mention time and again the expressions of affection: she embraces and kisses Jews of Saragossa, sends kisses to her grandson, and so on. She keeps her family ties with her Jewish relatives, the Cohens. And what is relevant here is that on one occasion some Jews had come to her house and *"they were talking about the Messiah who was to come"*. Gracia praised their words and said they were true. Again, what is important is this private setting in which the conversation of Jews turns to messianic matters.

IV

The learned astrological speculations connecting the Turkish victories with astral conjunctions have been studied often, on the basis of Hebrew theological writings. These speculations and interest were by no means restricted to the privileged space of learned Hebrew texts. Here again we are fortunate in having archival evidence of 'popular' oral statements. A few examples of this type of material may suffice here:[13] Yento Cubero testified on 2/8/1490, that, around 1481/2, while working at the house of Juan Ramírez de Lucena of Soria, some people

---

12. Op.cit., p. 142.
13. C. Carrete, *El Tribunal de la Inquisición en el Obispado de Soria (1486-1502)* (Salamanca, 1985), p. 22 # 9; p. 41 #59.

there where saying that the Turks were coming, and Yento Cubero said: "no, it is the Messiah who is coming". The wife of Juan Ramírez de Lucena said: "May it please God that the Messiah comes and that I should see it and after that [I would not mind even if] arrows came down from heaven and killed me."

Juan Ramírez de Lucena is an important figure in the Castilian history of the period and he has been associated with 'preerasmic' currents of thought.[14] In the Inquisition records he appears, though a Christian, as maintaining close contacts with Jewish relatives and Jewish townspeople. 'Yento' or Shem Tov seems, from his name, to be an artisan engaged in constructing barrels. Here we see notable figures of local society, associate with Jews and show their interest in messianic topics in their oral communications. Messianism was the subject of conversations, even in the town markets of Spain. From Inquisition records we learn that around 1473, Vidal Abenpesat and other Jews of Calatayud were talking with some *conversos* in the town market and the subject was "the coming of the Turks". The "coming of the Turk" is a subject which often appears in conversations about the Messiah. They show the political facet of Jewish and *converso* Messianism.

This evidence shows quite clearly that those messianic concerns which could be dismissed as 'only' and 'merely' *formulaic* were also real concerns articulated in *nonformulaic* and *nonpublic* occasions. They were not merely the concerns of learned texts bound by the rules of their literary genres. Nor were they articulated in Hebrew, language of the learned elite, but in the peninsular *romance*, accesible to all. The evidence opens up a new perspective for analyzing such Hebrew texts. All the more so since it may be argued that there is evidence of Jewish readings of Christian messianic texts in fifteenth century Spain. Indeed, an Inquisition testimony may be cited to this effect.

On the 12/1/1488 the son of Jacob Melamed, Antonio de Avila, sworn witness, testified before the Segovian Inquisition, about an event which transpired c. 1465: "He said that about twenty three years ago more or less this witness by [command of?] his father went to see Ysabel Arias, wife of the late Gómez Gonçalez de la Oz and [took to her] the story of King Ahasverus in a *megillah* written like a *Torah* and that this witness read it to her one night and a writing by fray Juan de Rozas

---

14. C. Carrete, 'Juan Ramírez de Lucena, judeoconverso del renacimiento español', in *Exile and Diaspora* (Jerusalem, 1991), 168-179.

Ysla in which it said that from the year sixty five would start the signs of the Antichrist and on the year seventy the world would end. And this witnesses' father had ordered Rabbi Za Aragonés to copy [*trasladar*] that text, because the Jews believed that it was then that the Messiah was to come."

If we are to reconstruct the event, we may say that a prominent Jewish family of Segovia, the Melamed family [Antonio de Avila may have been a Jew at that time] – at a time which, as we know from other sources, was a period of messianic speculation – was interested in Christian prophetic texts; that it had ordered their copy or translation and disseminated it by copying it and also by reading it. This was done presumably for comfort, on an appropiate day: *Purim*. But the testimony may be even more valuable. Who is the unidentified "fray Juan de Rozas Ysla" mentioned in the testimony? I would like to propose that we identify him with Juan de Rocatallada or Jean de Roquetaillade. Although Rocatallada is now the best known Spanish version of the friar's toponymic, one may recall that Peratallada, a village in the lower Ampurdam and seat of the Counts de Cruilles, used to be designated, in the eleventh to thirteenth centuries, as *Petra taliata, Petra incisa* or *Petra scisa,* possibly because of the great quarry in its vicinity. He was designated as *Petra-scissa.* The transition *Rocatallada/ Petrascisa* to *Rocascisa/Rozas Ysla* is easy to understand. If our identification is accepted, we have evidence, that amongst Jews, such as those in the Segovian circle we have mentioned, there was interest in, and dissemination of, the work of a bearer of the late mediaeval Joachimite millenarian tradition, who can, by no means, be described as 'marginal' or 'obscure'. Indeed, the famous disseminator of kabbalistic writings to the Christians, Pietro Columna or Petrus Galatinus, possessed his works; Postel derived from him his emphasis on the role of the French kings at the end of days; in sixteenth century Portugal, the popular *Trovas* of Bandarra with their promise of a 'hidden king' drew on his ideas; and so did Vieira's *Clavis Prophetarum*. Although the chief bearer of the Joachimite tradition in the Crown of Aragón may have been Arnau de Villanova, Roquetaillade had influenced the visions of the Infante Pedro de Aragón. Francesch Eiximenis uses his works when he describes the final victory of the 'Angelic Pope' and 'Good Emperor' in Jerusalem, and the 'conversion of the world' by the 'spiritual' Franciscans and Dominicans. Equally important is the work of an anonymous writer who authored the *Summula seu Breviloquium super concordia Novi et Vetuseris Testamenti* and who is probably, according to Reeves, a Catalonian Franciscan, writing c. 1368-70. The manuscript of this work (at the British Library) was copied for a merchant from Barcelona in 1455, and, later, given to a church there. Another copy, at the Vatican, was done in 1488. That is to say, that a work under the influence of Roquetaillade was still of interest at the time of the Jewish and *converso* messianic wave, that followed the conquest of Constantinople in the second half of the fifteenth century. Bignami-Odier studied the Catalan translations of Roquetaillade's *Liber Secretorum Eventum* and those of the *Vade mecum in tribulatione*. Indeed, his fame and influence in Catalonia, Castile and Portugal was so great that he was considered Catalan. He was born near Aurillac in the beginning of the fourteenth century. To this day he is used as a useful key to interpret the messianic prophecies of Arnaldo de Villanova. It may not be entirely fortuitous that the toponimic of the Jew who copied Rupescissa's work, Isaac Aragonés, points to the region where the Joachimite's works and influence were felt most strongly.

He believed that the House of Valois would create in Jerusalem a millenarian universal empire after the death of the Antichrist and with the help of the converted Jews. For him the Antichrist would be a Sicilian [Aragonese], would destroy the sect of Mohammed and expel the Moors from Spain and liberate the Holy Land. His Messianism has been described, by Reeves, as expressing a shift towards a renewed emphasis on secular events as portents in the eschatological scheme. One of the characteristics of his particular contribution was the order and timing of the events at the end of days. He shows a special interest in Spain. His prophetic scheme was clearly political and Reeves terms them 'convincingly simple in their range of black and white'. That is to say that they had all the ingredients to appeal to Jewish laymen in fifteenth century Spain. This is the type of Christian messianic literature which, if my proposition is correct, was available to Jews in Castilla la nueva in the generation of such Jews from Castile as Zacuto, Abravanel, Abraham b. Eleazar Ha-Levi, ibn Shraga, and also that of the circle of the *Sepher Ha-Meshiv*, etc.[15]

15. Marín, p. 86. For the transcription of Antonio de Avila's testimony see C. Carrete, *FIRC* III (Salamanca, 1986), No. 93 p. 58 (esp. nr. 9). On the Inquisition case of the Arias Dávila family see: E. Gutwirth, 'Elementos étnicos e históricos en las relaciones judeo-conversas en Segovia', *Jews and conversos* (Jerusalem, 1985), 83-102; id., 'On the Background to Cota's *Epitalamio Burlesco*', *Romanische Forschungen* 97, I (1985), 1-14; id., 'From Jewish to Converso Humour in Fifteenth Century Spain', *Bulletin of Hispanic Studies* LXVII (1990), 223-233;. id., 'Jewish-Converso Relations

in XVth C. Segovia', *Proceedings Eighth World Congress of Jewish Studies*, B (Jerusalem, 1982), 49-53. On Roquetaillade see M. Menéndez y Pelayo, *Historia de los Heterodoxos en España*, II (Madrid, 1947), p. 308ff; J. Bignami-Odier, *Etudes sur Jean de Roquetaillade* (Paris, 1952); A. Milhou, *Colón y su mentalidad mesiánica en el ambiente franciscanista español* (Valladolid, 1983), p. 383ff; M. Reeves, *The Influence of Prophecy in the Later Middle Ages. A Study in Joachimism* (Oxford, 1969); id. with Harold Lee and Giulio Silano, *Western Mediterranean Prophecy* (Toronto, 1989); id., *Joachim of Fiore and the Prophetic Future* (London, 1976). For 'trasladar' as 'copy' and 'translate' see Cobarruvias, *Tesoro*, s.v.

As background to this previously unknown Jewish and judaizing Segovian circle's interest in Joachimite prophetic texts, one may recall that Baer adduced evidence from the *Fortalitium Fidei* and from Inquisition cases in Valencia to the effect that the 1450's and onwards were a period of Messianic 'movements'. A number of writers have tried to repeat his work by compiling cases of emmigration to Jerusalem or Constantinople as evidence of Messianism. Needless to say not every case of emmigration to the Levant is proof of Messianic hope. Added to this, there seems to have been a certain scepticism even in the fifteenth century about the avowed 'Messianism' of these travellers. Hence the sarcastic remark of a Jew about a *converso* who wished to travel to Constantinople around 1459: 'if he had so much [money] it was not the Messiah he was seeking [in Jerusalem]' ['... et queste confesante... le respondio y se burlo del dicho maestre Abram diziendo que si el tenia tanto que no yria a buscar el mesias...]'. See Baer, *Die Juden* II, No. 410, p. 491. The manuscript, copied in his youth by Azariah dei Rossi (containing Hispano-Jewish Messianic speculations, recently published by Idel-Beth Arieh) contains statements that show the importance of the conjunction of the year 1464 to contemporaries. See M. Beth-Arieh and M. Idel, 'An Eschatological and Astrological Treatise by Abraham Zacuto (Hebrew)', *KS* LIV (1979), 191-194 (esp. 192, lines 30-31). Abravanel's views on 1464 (the time around which Segovian Jews ware reading Rocquetallada) as the beginning of a Messianic process are set forth in a number of passages of his work. See for example his Commentary on Ezequiel: "That is when [1464] the tribulations of the Jews *and their descendants* began... in Savoy and Provence and Piamonte and the whole of Lombardy and all the kingdoms of Spain, Sardinia, Sicily, Russia and the lands of the Emperor who inherited them from his father in Germany, Portugal, Navarre....". Evidently, some later elements are present in this late commentary, but the tradition of '1464-as-significant' seems to be earlier. See, for example, Y. Hacker, 'New Chronicles on the Expulsion of the Jews from Spain: its Causes and Effects (Hebrew)', *Zion* 44 (1979), pp. 201ff n.1. Scholem believed that Abravanel's position was one of 'constraint' by 'the dire misery and persecution' of his time. He had to admit apocalypse and popular mythology into his writings but allegorized eschatological writings. Since opposing tendencies of Jewish eschatology were merged in his writings 'everyone could find in them whatever best suited his temper', *Sabbetai Seri* (London, 1973), pp. 14-15. In view of the recent evidence it would be hard to retain this hypothesis of a sharp division between an 'apocalyptic eschatological Messianism characteristic of "the rabble" ' [ib. p. 14] and an 'aristocratic utopia' [ib.] typical of Maimonides and his followers. From a historical point of view it is not irrelevant that the apocalyptic 'rabble' includes some of the best minds of the Late Middle Ages and the Renaissance, and members of the Royal families and nobility of Castile and Aragón. Detailed attention to the documents in the peninsular *romance* does not allow the tendency of limiting Messianism to the *conversos*.

V

As we have seen political events are interpreted as signs of the messianic age before the Expulsion. The post-Expulsion texts written by Jews who were born in Spain, raised and educated there and which exhibit this characteristic may be seen as continuing a pre-Expulsion trend.

Another and quite different problem is that of the hypothetic political Messianism imagined by Castro. As might be recalled he spoke of the 'incitante profetismo de su casta judia' 'the prophetic incitations [to imperialism and world domination] of the Jewish caste'; of the 'represado y mesianico imperialismo', of the 'empresa de dominar el mundo tan insistentemente vaticinada por los conversos de Castilla'. It would therefore seem necessary to recall that there is a historical context for Hispano-Jewish messianic thought.

The Late Middle Ages in general have been seen as an epoch of millennarianism. To be sure the roots of the expressions of this sensibility were much older.[16] In the Greek Apocalypse of Pseudo-Methodius [c. end of the seventh century] one might find the source of the legend of the last days according to which a Greek or Roman emperor would vanquish the Moslems, would conquer Jerusalem and give over the empire to God at Golgotha. In the xvth century it was believed that Frederick II still lived and was waiting to reappear. The myth of the last emperor who vanquishes all religious and political enemies existed in Christian versions in Germany, France or in Italy. The new evidence on the Jewish conversations on the Turk serves to reinforce that adduced by Baer[17] to show the coincidence between Jewish and converso messianic hopes. But such a coincidence must also be analyzed, at least in part, by taking into account a European apocalyptic tradition in written texts which might form the context in a very wide sense of the interpretations of political events in messianic terms. There is also a Jewish tra-

---

16. Castro's views were repeatedly expounded and modified. See for example *Cervantes y los casticismos españoles* (Madrid, 1974), pp. 153-155, 199, 243. For the European context see the studies published in *The Use and Abuse of Eschatology in the Middle Ages,* ed. Werner Verbeke et al., *Mediaevalia Lovaniensia,* Studia XV (Leuven, 1988). MacKay, 'Andalucía y la guerra del fin del mundo', *Actas del V Coloquio international de historia medieval de Andalucía',* (s.l., s.d.), p. 332.

17. Y. Baer, 'The Messianic Movement in Spain during the period of the Expulsion' (Hebrew), *Zián* V (1936), 61-78; Y.Baer, *Historia de los judíos en la España cristiana,* vol. 2 (trad. J.L. Lacave) (Madrid,1981), cap.XI.

dition in esoteric texts which sees the end of days as connected with mythic apocalyptic clashes between Samael-Edom and the Messiah and its forces. This fight will precede the redemption.[18] These Jewish

18. J. Dan, 'The Beginnings of the Messianic Myth in Thirteenth Century Kabbalistic Thought (Hebrew)', *Messianism and Eschatology*, ed. Z. Baras (Jerusalem, 1983), 239-252 (p. 243). Isaac Ha Cohen had written that "the cantillation sign *yativ* [means] as it were that while the Jews [lit. Israel] are in decline [lit. go backwards] and are exterminated go backwards and not forwards, so [happens to] the hyposthasis of the upper hierarchies and this is what is written in the Ekha Scroll [Lam. 2/3] "He withdrew his right hand [when the enemy came on and he blazed in Jacob like flaming fire"] and the lowly bent ones shall become erect once again and the hypostasis of the right shall return to its source as it was at the beginning ... and then it shall come to pass as it is written 'love and truth justice and peace join hands, they have come together. Or, elsewhere: "*Qarnafukhiel...* in the future they shall bring the heffer in iron chains before *tif'eret* and before *malkhut* [the hyposthases glory and kingship] that is the Jewish people and this will bend down the rule of evil Edom these are the princes dressed in glory till the day of revenge. *Naqamiel, Harviel, Shalshiel* their mnemonic symbol is *nahash*-serpent and when our just Messiah, he who is likened unto a serpent, shall come, the serpent shall come and will take its revenge from the serpent ... and the fish whose name is *Yanun* shall come and swallow the fish whose name is *Dagdagiron*.' In Isaac Ha-Cohen's *Treatise on the Left handed Emmanation* he writes that '... from intercourse of [the devil Ashmodai] and [the she-devil] Lilith was born a great prince / archeon in heaven who rules over eighty thousand destroyers and he is called the sword of king Ashmodai'. One may note that the ichtyic symbolism we find in a Jewish gnostic such as Isaac Ha Cohen was not a privative feature. It was by no means uncommon in Christian Messianic texts in fifteenth century Spain: the third sign of the imminence of the end of the world in Martín Martínez de Ampiés' *Libro del Antichristo* is that 'the fishes of the sea will rise and cry out in anguish'. Oral folk literature preserved similar metaphors in the *Romancero del Rey Rodrigo*.(Milhou, op. cit., p. 467). For Palencia's description of the Andalusian beliefs in Leviathan in the second half of the fifteenth century see infra. Eschatological battles involving mythical beasts are common in the Christian Spanish (perhaps particularly in Catalonian texts), prophetic Messianic traditions from Villanova to Alamany. A further example of such ideas (eschatological battles, mythical beasts, massive conversions, etc.) in late mediaeval texts in Catalan would be the prophecies of fra Anselm Turmeda ed. by Ramon d'Alos in *Revue Hispanique* 24 (1911), pp.480-496. It is noteworthy from our point of view that the manuscript of the prophecies at the Carpentras Library which serves the apparatus of that edition contains also the prophecies of Ioan de Rocatallada. (Cf. ibid. p. 481). See also A. Raimondi, 'Les Profecies di Anselmo Turmeda', *Archivio Storico per la Sicilia Orientale* XI (1914), 232-249. There are also prophecies made by the ass in his dialogue with the mule on which see M. de Riquer, *Historia de la literatura catalana* (Barcelona, 1980), pp. 296ff. For the view that the writings of kabbalists such as Chiquitilla reflect an attitude towards Christianity which is that of the Spanish Jews of his time and place see R. Goetschel, 'Le motif des Sarim dans les écrits de Joseph Giqatilia' in *Michael* XI, ed. E. Gutwirth, with S. Simonsohn (Tel Aviv, 1989), 9-32.

gnostics expressed the sufferings of exile in Spain, their desire for vengeance against the gentiles, and a mythical vision of redemption and the coming of the Messiah. There is no reason to doubt that their allusions were expressions of hopes about real political rulers even if their actual names are not mentioned. By the fifteenth century there were Jews who in their conversations expressed similar ideas – i.e. the messianic interpretations of past or recent political events – though not necessarily in gnostic terms. There is, in the fifteenth century, an intensification and diffusion of the basic sentiments we found in thirteenth century texts. An ever increasing amount of Hebrew evidence also supports this view. Added to this is the realization that a significant number of post-Expulsion Jewish Messianists had either grown up or matured in the Spain of the Catholic Monarchs. This phenomenon should be seen also against the background of its spiritual landscape, that is to say against the background of fifteenth century Spanish Christian Messianism and apocalyptics rather than, say, Italian analogues or sixteenth century ones of doubtful relevance. A number of genres have preserved evidence of the existence of such a Christian background to those Jewish learned and popular messianic ideas we have mentioned above: popular anonymous *romances*; poetic historiography (i.e verses about contemporary events) as well as messianic letters emmanating from the circles of the nobility close to Ferdinand. In the analysis of these texts the precise fifteenth century Hispano-Jewish and converso mentality has not been taken into consideration. A vague suprahistorical and 'essential' Jewish Messianism has been taken for granted. On the other hand, students of the Hebrew texts have not always paid as much attention to this Christian context and analogues as to other aspects. Part of the problem may lie in that a number of items of such evidence have only recently been brought to light, collected, dated, transcribed or paraphrased. Most frequently such pieces of evidence have been studied independently of each other. And yet a number of concrete features are common to these various strands. Even more important may be an unquantifiable *donnée*: the quality of intensity shared by them.

Pedro de Marcuello, a Castilian poet of the reign of the Catholic Monarchs, might be a good example.[19] The point of view of his politi-

---

19. *Cancionero de Pedro de Marcuello*, ed. J.M. Blecua (Zaragoza, 1987); Michel García, 'El cancionero de Pero Marcuello', *The Age of the Catholic Monarchs 1474-1516. Literary Studies in Memory of Keith Whinnom* (Liverpool, 1989), p. 55 and Pedro Cátedra, *La historiografía en verso en la época de los Reyes Católicos: Juan Barba y su Consolatoria de Castilla* (Salamanca, 1989).

cal verse is messianic and prophetic. He cites prophecies of Pseudo-Isidore about Spain. He speaks of the prince who will unify the world and conquer Jerusalem: "and prophecies have been found saying that they shall go to Jerusalem victorious and joyous…" "y fallanse profecias/ con vitoria y alegrias/iran a Jherusalen." Further evidence may be found in an anonymous romance of c. 1484. It expresses the belief that the Catholic Monarchs "shall win the Holy House / as has been prophesied/ and shall hang on the Holy Sepulchre/ their flag/" "ganen la Casa santa/ segun es profetizado/ y pongan al Santo Sepulcro/ su rreal pendon cruzado". Another *romance* may be adduced: it exhorts the Monarchs: "as the Scripture says / and as the holy ones have prophesied/ you are the monarchs/ of whom God will make use/ march on emperors/ you shall visit the Holy Sepulchre…" "Segun dizen escrituras/ y de santos profecia/ que vos reyes sois aquellos/ de quien Dios se sirvia/ Caminad emperadores //visitareis el Sepulcro".[20] Juan Barba is another author of this period. He wrote a long historical poem recently published by Pedro Cátedra. It was written during the time of the Catholic monarchs and in their honour. He is a good example of the providentialist trend at the time of the Catholic Monarchs. A comet which was seen in his time is interpreted as a sign that God had chosen the monarchs: "The great secret which superior Providence kept/ has been brought by that comet" "El grande secreto qu'estava guardado / de la Providencia superiora/ aquella cometa lo truxo a la ora/ y el curso del tienpo lo ha demostrado". Barba's universe is apocalyptic: 'saligia' the beast [acronym of the seven cardinal sins] reigns. His Copla 318 reads:

20. *Cancionero Musical de Palacio,* ed. J. Romeu Figueras (Barcelona, 1965), No. 143 and P. Cátedra, op. cit. In 1489 Juan Anchieta wrote a romance to be sung at the royal chapel which contains the following lines: "you shall visit the Holy Sepulchre with joy… the Roman Pontifex shall crown you…" (Milhou, op. cit., p. 386). In an eschatological treatise Joseph ibn Shraga, the Spanish Kabbalist from Castile (cf. Isaiah Tishby, *Messianism in the Time of the Expulsion from Spain and Portugal,* Jerusalem, 1985, p. 133) asserted that in 1512 the Temple would be rebuilt and sacrifices would again be offered there. The beliefs that the period preceding the Expulsion was a Messianic period expressed by Abravanel, Zacuto, and many other Iberian Jews born, raised and matured in the fifteenth century have been frequently mentioned. For the existence of 'a whole corpus of kabbalistic writings deeply immersed in Messianic hopes, expectations and redemptive activity' contemporary, it would seem with the war with Granada, in the writings of the circle of the *Sepher ha-Meshiv,* cf. M. Idel, 'Religion, Thought and Attitudes: the Impact of the Expulsion on the Jews' in *Spain and the Jews,* ed. E. Kedourie (London, 1992), 123-139 (p. 128). See also M. Idel, 'The attitude to Christianity in the *Sepher Ha-Meshiv* (Hebrew) ', *Zián* XLVI/2 (1981), 77-91, who maintains that the *Sepher Ha-Meshiv* contains direct adaptations of Christian doctrine on the divinity and virgin birth of the Messiah. The book's idea that Christendom

"and of this king it was said by the ancients that he was *omis omo* will all his kingship" "Y deste tal rey antigos dixeron/ ser omis omo con toda su alteza". Ferdinand is the 'man of men'[21].

I would suggest that all these texts should be borne in mind when analyzing the various Jewish messianic texts of this place and period.[22]

This spiritual landscape would have to include the idea that Spain was somehow at the centre or closely connected to the events of the end of days. It is implicit in the Jewish oral comments about the Turks coming to Spain which I have cited above from Inquisition records. It underlies similar ideas expressed in Hebrew texts. Such Jewish ideas had a Christian counterpart. One example might be Fray Johan Alamany's *Treatise* possibly written in the first half of the xvth century. It was translated into Catalan by Johan Carbonell, was printed, probably in Barcelona, at the end of the xvth century. In it we read passages such as "When the beast of Spain shall be sixteen years it will begin to rise and there will be great destruction most of it will be destroyed till the *encubert* /hidden one will save all the Christians. And the hidden one shall destroy all the moors in Spain and all the Jews and the forced converts will be dealt with cruelly because they are deceivers scorners and are contemptuous of the faith of Jesus Christ... and he shall strengthen and help the New David ...and he shall come with many lions unicorns and elephants ...to clean the land of all the dirt or impurity that is on it." In other words, even the fact that there is a mythical component in the articulation of messianic ideas is not an exclusively Jewish characteristic of messianic thinking. Alamany's 'beast of Spain' or Barba's

---

would undergo conversions to Judaism at the time preceeding the final redemption of the Jews is reminiscent of the emphasis on conversion in the writings of Turmeda or Allamany. The secret sciences which are revealed in the book are understood in it as secrets which are to be revealed to the Jews on the eve of the Messianic era. According to Idel the eschatological events implied in the ninth book are crucial for understanding that kabbalistic literature. The ninth 'lost book of Solomon' which he is revealing contains 'the secret of the nine spheres and how they will be connected to each other when the Messiah will come and the Supernal Jerusalem will descend'. See M. Idel's paper to the Congress on the Three Cultures at Toledo: 'Magic and Mysticism in the Book of the Responding Entity' [typescript].

21. Pedro Cátedra, *La historiografía en verso en la época de los Reyes Católicos: Juan Barba y su Consolatoria de Castilla* (Salamanca, 1989), p. 25, n. 24-26, 29, 51, 77, 111, p. 30, 33, 47 etc.

22. A. Milhou, *Colón y su mentalidad mesiánica en el ambiente franciscanista español* (Valladolid, 1983). But see also J. Gil, *Mitos y utopías del Descubrimiento* (Madrid, 1989), pp.193-223.

Saligia may not be identical with Yanin or Dagdagiron but they are all examples of the use of marvelous beasts or creatures in the mythic language of Messianism in Spain. Such beliefs are not exclusive to eccentric millenarians but are much more widely held, as reported by contemporary chroniclers. Díez de Games, chronicler of Pero Niño would write: "And if you think about it, as soon as there is a new king they make a new Merlin. They say that that king will go across the sea and kill all the Moors and conquer the holy House and will be Emperor; that is what used to be said by the people in the past and that is what they shall say in the future." As is well known, Columbus had written that "the abbot Joachim, the Calabrian, said that from Spain would come out he who would rebuild the house on Mount Zion."[23] We have argued that a number of traditions merge in the Messianism of fifteenth century Spain. This Jewish Messianism was commensurate in some aspects with Christian counterparts. Its foci were the coming of the Turks and the war with Granada.

VI

If this new perspective on Hispano-Jewish Messianism is accepted that is to say, if we are to look to the historic background – i.e. the Spanish fifteenth century background – we must be able to analyze even fairly esoteric Hebrew texts in a somewhat different light. A recently published manuscript would be a good and final example. One may pay attention to this concrete Hebrew text and see in what ways it parallels Jewish oral and Christian beliefs.[24]

Cambridge Genizah fragment T-S K 22/12 contains a treatise of what has been described as messianic propaganda. Internal evidence reveals that it was written in Egypt, in 1501, probably around March. The author had prophetic visions and used the *gymatria* method as well as astrological calculations, automatic writing and, at times, had his inspiration in an ecstatic state while his head was held between his

---

23. MacKay, op. cit.; Milhou, op. cit.; G. Diez de Games, *El Vistorial*, ed. J. de Mata Carriazo (Madrid, 1940), p. 69.

24. Isaiah Tishby, *Messianism in the Time of the Expulsion from Spain and Portugal* (Hebrew) (Jerusalem, 1985). Joseph ibn Shraga's treatise on the end of days written in 1499 relates eschatological expectations to the Spanish experiences of the fifteenth century (p. 132). On the exaltation of Ferdinand as the eschatological emperor see Milhou, op. cit., ch. 2/5 and 3/5.

knees. It was not published but apparently consigned to the Genizah. There is no doubt that this is a highly individualistic, some would say eccentric writer. Nevertheless the points of contact with other textual Jewish traditions are well documented by Tishby. What might still need to be added are the nonliterary Hispano-Jewish and the Hispanic Christian backgrounds. There is no doubt of the strong current of Hispanicity that runs through the book. The author imposes Spanish syntax on his Hebrew linguistic constructions. He searches biblical texts for the numerical equivalences of years in the Gregorian calendar and the events of Spanish and Iberian history are seen as portents of the coming of the Messiah.

In addition to these examples of the Hispanicity of the anonymous author of the Genizah fragment there are two points I should like to emphasize here. The first is the regional factor. As has been noticed concrete references to places in Spain in the text are related to Andalusia. Sevile is the only Spanish town mentioned by name. His spelling of /Os Estaos/ as /Los estaos/ may be of interest: the use of /los/ instead of /os/ is, of course, a sign of his non Portuguese origin as noted by Tishby. In addition the weakening of the intervocalic /d/ is typical of Andalusia. Assuming then, that the author is andalusian, or that his messianic interpretations of current events is focused on Andalusia we might benefit from relating the work of this writer to the spiritual currents which were thought to be characteristic of Andalusia. That is to say that in reading the Genizah text we should bear in mind the perception of regional beliefs in Andalusia in the second half of the fifteenth century expressed by a contemporary such as Alonso de Palencia. He believed that "the people who had these beliefs were for the most part andalusians who are given to such imaginings ...about the supposed appearance of Leviathan." Nor is such an association between andalusians and messianic ideas exclusive to Palencia. The *Libro del Alborayque* contains similar views: "Let us see why they are called false prophets thus is called he who believes in lies about the future ...the prophets prophesied that the Messiah would come to Jerusalem at an appointed time a time, which has passed. They [the conversos?] say that he shall come to Sevile or to Lisbon and that he is yet to come ...also Zacariah says that the Messiah will come to Jerusalem as a humble knight on a mule... they say that he shall come to Sevile, as an emperor, as a rich knight on a chariot of gold. They say he shall come to kill the Christians by the sword and [these are] false prophets who prophesy against the true prophets".25

The second point concerning the thought of the anonymous author of the Genizah fragment, is his vision of Spanish events as having particular relevance to universal history. As we have seen this is a feature of the messianic perceptions of Hispanic Jews and Hispanic Christians such as Alamany and of those messianic ideas described by Palencia, Díez de Games, and the *Alborayque*. But there is a further point of contact. Here I should like to pay attention to his focusing on King Ferdinand as a personality who is closely connected to the messianic process.

Thus the Genizah text sees Ferdinand as being particularly relevant to the messianic process: [p. 20] "I found that it was under the sign of *naval* that Ferdinand expelled the Jews from Sevile". The numerical value of the word *naval* [Ps 14/1 and 53/2:] "The impious fool [says in his heart there is no God] is 82" [i.e. 1482]. The Hebrew Bible, then, according to the author of the Genizah treatise refers to Ferdinand and to the Gregorian calendar. Another relevant passage: "[p. 21] the communities gave Ferdinand 18000 *castellanos* every year to finance the war with the Moors this is according to the sign [Dan 12 /7] "when the power of the holy people ceases to be dispersed all these things shall come to an end -w-ke-khalot [=when it ceases] is equal to the numerical value of 482 [i.e. 1482]". Again [p. 6a/ p. 67] "and for that reason [i.e. for the persecutions in Spain] the whole world shall be troubled ....and about that it was said in Daniel [2/34]" While you looked a stone was hewn from a mountain not by human hands'; it struck the image on its feet of iron and clay and shattered them. Here [the Bible] alluded to the king Ferdinand [by using] the expression *parzela*..." [=iron =fierro=ferran].

For the author of the Genizah fragment the figure of Ferdinand looms large in messianic thinking. As we have seen earlier this is not exclusive to him no matter how individual or eccentric one might think him. It would seem then that there was a sense in which messianic

---

25. A. Mackay, 'Andalucía y la guerra del fin del mundo', *Actas del V Coloquio international de historia medieval de Andalucia,* 329-42; N. López Martinez, *Los judaizantes castellanos y la Inquisición en tiempos de Isabel la Católica* (Burgos, 1954), p. 393.

ideas in the Spain of the seventies and the eighties focused on Ferdinand. The association of Ferdinand in particular with messianic processes should, I would suggest, be seen against the background of Spanish beliefs of the 1480's: beliefs of nobles, of intellectuals and of the people at large These are the beliefs which may be reconstructed from such evidence as the oral utterances recorded in Inquisition files, anonymous popular romance of 1484, the currency of pseudo-Isidore's prophecies at that time and place, the writings of Pero Marcuello, Juan Barba's verses and Johan Carbonell's translation of Alamany's treatise.26

26. A further example of the anonymous Hispano-Jewish author's particular attitude to the symbolism of vernacular onomastics – in our case that of Ferdinand – is to be found on f. 6b of the T-S MS. He refers [ed. Tishby, p. 120 lines 20-21] to Ps 2, a Messianic text. But he interprets verse 9: "You shall break them with a rod of iron; you shall shatter them like a clay pot," (a promise against the 'nations who furiously rage together... the kings of the earth [who] stand ready... the rulers [who] conspire together...') as a reference to the Kingdom of Ferdinand [whose name means 'iron']. The repeated use of Spanish onomastic symbolism may be significant. Attention to onomastic symbolism in Spain at this period seems to have been intensified. Francesch Eiximenis for example thinks it significant that the name of St John [Johannes] begins with J and finishes with S like the name of Jesus; Hernando del Pulgar, in his epistle to the 'doctor of Talavera' c. 1478, plays on the fact that the recently born prince Juan is homonymous to St. John in whose day the lesson read at Church is Messianic; Christopher Columbus' thought his name XPO Ferens was highly significant; Las Casas says that Divine Providence names its messengers with names which accord with their purpose or calling; Hernando Colón interpreted his father's first name as revealing of his mission: he who brings or takes for Christ. Cf. Milhou, op. cit., p. 58 n.128 and ff. See also pp. 361, 363 for the symbolism of Ferdinand amongst the Christians who saw significance in the homonimity with Ferdinand III de Castilla y León. It may be equally significant that the cult of this Ferdinand is associated – like the anonymous author of the Genizah fragments – with late mediaeval Andalusia. In 1476 the Catalan Pedro Azamar, doctor of the law and counsellor of Juan II, had said about Ferdinand that his name meant fortress and was therefore related to a Joachimite Messianic prophecy [ib. p. 364]. Rabbi Solomon b. Samuel Ha-Sefardi also sees significance in the symbolism of his name when he writes about Ferdinand in his elegy to the exiled Jews from Spain: 'the king of iron [barzel] he is Nimrod, he is Amarphel...'. See the edition by A. Freimann in *Festschrift Zwi Perez Hayyus* (Vienna, 1933), pp. 237-239 and Hacker, loc. cit. (n. 58).

Hyam Maccoby

THE TORTOSA DISPUTATION, 1413-14, AND ITS EFFECTS

Of all the Jewish-Christian Disputations, that of Tortosa was organised on the largest and most ambitious scale; and it was also the most successful in achieving missionary aims. The key figure in promoting the Disputation was Vicente Ferrer, later canonized as a saint. An understanding of the role of Vicente Ferrer will provide one of several important links between the Tortosa Disputation and the Expulsion of the Jews which took place about eighty years later.

Two previous public Disputations provided a fund of experience, both positive and negative, for the organisers of the Tortosa Disputation. These were the Paris Disputation of 1240, and the Barcelona Disputation of 1263. Both these earlier Disputations centred on the Talmud, the body of teachings that comprised the ongoing discussions and decisions of rabbinic Judaism in its centuries-long contemplation of the Hebrew Bible and the application of biblical commandments to the problems of everyday life. As well as these legal discussions and decisions (*halakhah*), the Talmud contained much meditation on the theological aspects of the Biblical narrative, as well as stories and moral sayings of post-biblical teachers (*aggadah*). The Talmud, in fact, together with its associated rabbinic writings (the Midrashic literature) and the later commentaries and compositions of rabbis down to the time of the Disputations themselves (including the Geonim, Maimonides, Rashi and the Tosafists), governed the religious life of medieval Jews in the same way as Christian religious life was based not on the bare New Testament texts but on the institutions, councils and post-biblical literature (patristic and postpatristic) of the Church. Yet the importance of the Talmud to the Jews was, for a long time, very little understood by Christians, and when finally understood came as a considerable shock. It was the new understanding of the importance of the Talmud that led to a change in policy towards the conversion of the Jews, including the organisation of the Disputations.

The beginning of sustained Christian awareness of the Talmud can be dated to the letter of Pope Gregory IX written in 1239. In this he addresses the leaders of Christendom on the subject, stating that the Talmud is "the most important reason why the Jews remain obstinate in their perfidy", requiring them to seize all copies of the Talmud. This followed the secession of Nicholas Donin from Judaism. Donin became a Franciscan friar, and he addressed letters to the Pope alerting him to the alleged heresies, blasphemies and obscenities contained in the Talmud. The Pope's letter already shows that Talmudic Jews are being distinguished sharply from Biblical Jews. Only the latter are to be included in the designation of practisers of a "licit" religion. Talmudic Jews, on the contrary, since they show allegiance not just to the Bible but to a post-Biblical heretical work, the Talmud, are to be regarded as heretics. The definition of "heretics" is in Christian terms; i.e. belief in the authority of the Talmud constitutes a heresy not of Judaism but of Christianity, and can thus, in theory, come under the jurisdiction of the Inquisition. As a "licit" religion, Judaism was regarded as a branch of Christianity, and therefore as liable to Christian regulation. The Pope thus claims the authority to decide which kind of Judaism is allowed or "licit", and which is disallowed as heretical[1].

An important gloss is thus announced on the dictum of Augustine (*De civitate Dei*, 18: 46, 20:29) by which the status of Jews and Judaism in Christendom had hitherto been defined. Augustine had pronounced that the Jewish religion was to be permitted, and not stamped out as heresy, since the Jews, by practising their religion, provided ocular proof of the truth of Christianity, both by confirming the New Testament picture of the Judaism out of which Christianity arose, and on whose prophecies it was based, and also, through their miserable and subjected condition, confirming the truth of the supersession of Judaism by Christianity. Implied in this Augustinian doctrine, however, was that Judaism was to be preserved as a kind of fossil. Jews were to be Old Testament Jews, so that they could act as a foil to New Testament Christians. But the idea of Judaism as on ongoing, developing religion was ruled out. Thus the Talmud, embodying as it did the unpalatable fact that the Jewish religion was still alive and in progress of development, and that the Jewish Synagogue, like the Church, claimed continuous power of decision on current issues, contradicted the whole Augustinian picture of Old Testament Jews, and had to be condemned as heretical. In fact, the Jews even in the time of Jesus ware not Old Testament Jews, since rabbinic Judaism had already been producing far-reaching developments ever since the time of Ezra. The Talmud

---

1. Pope Gregory IX's letter was followed by similar pronouncements by the succeeding Popes, Innocent IV, Alexander IV, Clement IV and John XXII.

already existed, though in oral and relatively undeveloped form, in the time of Jesus, as the New Testament itself attests, when it speaks of the traditions of the Pharisees and of their authority as those who sit "in Moses' seat" (Mat.23:2). But Pharisaism (though with some inconsistencies) is condemned in the New Testament, which thus foreshadows the distinction made by the Church between Old Testament Jews and Talmudic Jews.

Nevertheless, the Talmud came as a surprise to Pope Gregory, though several Christian writers in the previous century (including Peter Alfonsi and Peter the Venerable) had already referred to the Talmud in a minor way in their polemics against Judaism. The first substantial Christian reaction to the Pope's initiative was embodied in the Disputation of Paris (1240), in which Nicholas Donin himself accused the Talmud, which was defended by Rabbi Yehiel of Paris[2]. No positive qualities were perceived in the Talmud by the Christian side, and the upshot of the debate was that the Talmud was totally condemned and an attempt was made to extirpate it by burning all copies that could be found.

Soon, however, a new and more sophisticated Christian reaction to the Talmud arose, associated especially with the Dominican movement, and with its great leader, Raymund de Penaforte. In this new policy, the Talmud was not wholly condemned. On the contrary, it was argued that certain passages in the Talmud and Midrash attest the truth of Christianity (even this approach had been briefly anticipated by Peter Alfonsi). At the Barcelona Disputation it had not yet been explained how this mixture of truth and falsehood came to exist in the Talmud. A theory of the Talmud as consisting of several layers, of which the earlier ones contained prophetic truth, and the later rabbinic falsehood, was later developed in the thought of Raymund Martini, author of *Pugio Fidei*, and was used explicitly in the Tortosa Disputation. In the Barcelona Disputation, however, the negative aspects of the Talmud are not mentioned. Only the positive (i.e. allegedly pro-Christian) aspects are employed, in an attempt to convert Jews to Christianity through their own revered writings, in a manner somewhat similar

---

2. An earlier case of interference in Jewish religious life was the Christian censoring of the works of Maimonides during the Maimonidean controversy. The details of this affair (which took place in Montpellier in 1232 or 1234) are much disputed, but it seems that some Jewish anti-Maimunists denounced Maimonides's philosophical works as heretical to the Christian authorities.

to the way the Old Testament was used in missionary activity. This did not mean, of course, that the organisers of the Barcelona Disputation had given up the accusations against the Talmud as blasphemous and obscene. These accusations, which had formed the core of the Paris Disputation, were revived shortly after the Barcelona Disputation in the enquiry into the Talmud instituted by Papal decree[3]. Finally, in the Tortosa Disputation, about 150 years later, the two lines of attack, positive and negative, were combined in a single disputation.

The new positive approach to certain aspects of the Talmud was thus by no means an acknowledgment of the Talmud as a valid continuation of the Old Testament for Jews. On the contrary, what was now being said was that certain Talmudic passages belonged to the authoritative nexus of the Old Testament itself, being valid traditions dating either from biblical times or from Jewish circles sympathetic to Christianity; while the vast bulk of Talmudic sayings were late and worthless, being the productions of a rabbinic movement which had no right to exist since it defiantly denied the authority of Christ and the Church.

The great missionizing campaign directed towards the Jews in Spain began with Raymund de Penaforte and the Barcelona Disputation which he organised (though the Christian spokesman was Pablo Christiani), and culminated in the Tortosa Disputation which was based on 150 years of effort on the lines which he initiated. It was stimulated by the Christian discovery of the Talmud, and it involved strenuous Christian study of the Talmudic literature in order both to use it and to combat it. But in effect, this effort was not aimed at returning the Jews to the status of Old Testament Jews, as Augustine had envisaged them when he declared Judaism be a tolerated religion. Such an aim may still have played a part in the Paris Disputation, when the burning of the Talmud was intended to cause the Jews to revert to the Old Testament. But later it seems to have been understood that the picture of Old Testament Jews was an illusion, and the only Jews who really existed were Talmudic Jews. This realisation meant that the old basis of toleration had been destroyed. The new missionary campaign aimed at the conversion of Jews to Christianity, not at returning them to a fossilized state which had existed only in Christian minds. Once the new conception had arisen, there was no turning back. The only possibility left was

---

3. This took place in 1264 under the chairmanship of Raymund de Penaforte, with the specific commission to examine the Talmud for blasphemy.

of a Christendom that contained no Jews. Since Spain was the scene of operation of this new concept, the expulsion of the Jews from Spain became a real possibility. There was no longer room for practising Jews in Christian society, once it was fully understood what being a practising Jew meant. Only those Jews who opted for conversion to Christianity could escape expulsion.

It may be argued, however, that Christian hostility to the Talmud was not as great as the above argument represents. Surely the tactics used by Geronimo de Santa Fé (formerly Joshua Halorki) on the Christian side of the Tortosa Disputation show considerable respect for the Talmud. For when the Jewish participants refused to accept as authoritative certain Talmudic or Midrashic passages quoted by Geronimo, he indignantly accused them of heresy, since, as he asserted, orthodox Judaism required them to accept everything in the Talmudic writings. This paradoxical situation, in which the Christian disputant appears to champion the Talmud against its own adherents, requires explanation. Whereas in previous disputations, the Talmud had been attacked by Christians as a heretical work, here the Jews were being declared guilty of heresy because of their lack of belief in the Talmud. The paradox, however, is easily resolved. The Talmud was regarded (apart from a few passages) as embodying a heresy of Christianity; but Geronimo was accusing the Jews of lacking consistency in being heretical in terms of Talmudic Judaism itself. Not only were Christians claiming to decide what kind of Judaism was a Christian heresy; they were here even claiming to decide what was heretical within Judaism. Though Christians, who rejected the authority of the Talmud, claimed the right to distinguish between what was valid and what was invalid in it, they argued that Jews, who accepted the Talmud's authority, had no such right. The Jewish disputants, however, pointed out that though they accepted the Talmud's authority, Jewish theory had always distinguished between degrees of authority in the rabbinic writings, regarding *aggadic* passages as less authoritative and more open to variety of interpretation than *halakhic* passages, and minority opinions recorded in the Talmud as less weighty than majority opinions.

The Tortosa Disputation thus summed up the work of the Dominican scholars since the thirteenth century on how to cope with the place occupied by the Talmud in the minds and hearts of the Jews whom they hoped to convert, while the Jewish participants made use of considerable experience in combating a form of missionizing that focussed more on the Talmud than on the prophecies of the Hebrew Bible.

The Tortosa Disputation was organised on a magnificent scale. Even though the two previous public Disputations, those of Paris and Barcelona, were both royal occasions, being presided over respectively by Queen Blanche of Castile, mother of Louis IX, and King James of Aragon, the Tortosa Disputation was a much more lavish affair. Instead of lasting a few days, it lasted for 69 sessions over a period of twenty-one months. Instead of being commemorated, on the Christian side, by a brief communique, it was the subject of voluminous "protocols" or minutes kept session by session by the papal notary, and comprising over 600 pages in the edition of Pacios Lopez (1957). The chairman of the Disputation was one who was regarded, at least by himself, as greater than any king, the Pope Benedict XIII, whose claim to the papacy, however, was eventually rejected by the Council of Constance. Representatives of all the Jewish communities of Aragon and Catalonia were summoned to take part, while seventy seats were provided for cardinals, archbishops and bishops and accommodation for nearly a thousand Church dignitaries. According to the Hebrew account, when the Jewish participants entered the scene of the Disputation, " ...our heart melted and became water: nevertheless we made the blessing, 'Blessed is he who has apportioned some of his glory to flesh and blood'."

This immense expenditure is itself symptomatic of the all-out effort that went into the Dominican campaign to convert the Jews. The Augustinian status of Judaism as a 'licit' religion had not excluded sporadic attempts to convert Jews to Christianity. Some of the *Adversus Judaeos* literature was directed to this end, though even more of it was intended for the consumption of Christian readers who needed to be reassured in their faith. But the new all-out effort implies that a new urgency was felt in converting the Jews. One important reason for this has already been outlined: the erosion of the illusory picture of the Jews as Old Testament figures who could be safely left in a state of suspended animation as witnesses to the Judaism of ancient times. The Talmud as chief evidence of a living, developing Judaism thus became the target. But there were also other important factors that gave urgency to the need to convert the Jews, and contributed to the development of a crisis in which there was no alternative to the ultimatum - either convert, or be expelled.

Vicente Ferrer was one of the chief influences of the times in Spain, and he had been partly instrumental in bringing about the Tortosa Disputation. While the Disputation was proceeding, he was reinforcing its message by visiting the Jewish communities of Aragon and Castile (in the absence of their rabbis at the Disputation) with a conversion message in which threats played a large part. The disoriented and terrified communities responded by providing hundreds of converts, who were brought by Ferrer to the Disputation itself to proclaim their conversion day by day at the beginning of the sessions.

Ferrer was a figure of great significance. He embodied the pristine ideals of the mendicant orders which had been created in the thirteenth century with a specific mission to combat heresy. Saint Dominic himself had begun his career by wandering among the Albigensian heretics in an effort to bring them back to the Catholic fold. The mendicant orders, with their vow of poverty, and their itinerant life, showed the ideal of a return to primitive spirituality in the face of disintegrative threats to the Church. In a sense, they emulated the zeal of the heretics, showing a reaction against the settled wealth and sloth of the monastic orders, which had themselves originally aimed at renewal. Thus the mendicant orders had always been connected with ideas that at least bordered on the apocalyptic. Notions of millenarianism, involving expectations of the imminent Second Coming of Christ, his battle against the Antichrist, and his earthly reign, were often associated with groups that rebelled against the Church, but this was not always the case. Many orthodox churchmen were also the purveyors of apocalyptic ideas, and these were especially prevalent among the friars, who were both within the Establishment and outside it. Raymund Lull (d. 1315), for example, the great Franciscan missionary, lived in constant expectation of the End of Days and the Last Judgment. The Franciscan Spirituals were a great source of mystical apocalyptic writings in the 13th and 14th centuries. In especial, the apocalyptic scheme of the visionary Joachim of Fiore was influential in orthodox as well as in heretical circles.

Vicente Ferrer is a prime example of the apocalyptic fervour associated with the more radical side of the mendicant orders. His sermons continually prophesied the imminence of the Parousia and the Day of Judgment. He himself claimed to have had a vision supporting this belief. He was accompanied in his travels by bands of flagellants. The phenomenon of flagellant asceticism, especially when performed in public by travelling ecstatic bands, was strongly associated with millenarian hopes. Vicente Ferrer can thus be regarded as typical of the form of mendicant missionary activity that was linked to apocalypticism.

This element of apocalypticism may afford further explanation of the new urgency in the missionary campaign to convert the Jews. There has been some disagreement among modern scholars about whether the Dominican and Franciscan campaigns to convert the Jews should be regarded as a radical departure from the Church's previous Augustinian policy towards the Jews. Jeremy Cohen has argued that it was, while Robert Chazan has disagreed, arguing that St. Augustine, while giving Judaism "licit" status, had never attempted to discourage efforts to bring the Jews within the Christian fold. When the element of apocalypticism is taken into account, however, this disagreement can be resolved. St. Augustine certainly had the intention, by his doctrine of a "licit" Judaism, to discourage missionary efforts to some extent. For his doctrine put the Jews into a different category from heretics, such as the Albigensians, who had to be given a stark choice between conversion or death. Yet St. Augustine, as Chazan says correctly, by no means gave up the hope of the eventual conversion of the Jews. On the contrary, this hope could never be abandoned because the conversion of the Jews had been directly prophesied by St. Paul in Romans 11. But Paul's prophecy was linked to his vision of the End of Days. The conversion of the Jews as a whole was regarded as an apocalyptic event, though individual Jews might be converted before that. Thus when Christians thought of the Apocalypse as far off in the future, the Augustinian doctrine of a "licit" Judaism was paramount. But when apocalyptic hopes became strong or desperate, the other attitude towards the Jews came to the fore. The "licit" status of Judaism was always an essentially interim conception, pending the final solution of all things at the End of Days. Thus there is no contradiction between the Augustinian attitude and that of mendicant apocalyptists such as Vicente Ferrer. Augustine lived at a time when the End of Days seemed far off. Vicente Ferrer, however, saw around him the signs of the coming total triumph of Christianity: the growing power of the Papacy and the defeat of Islam. Recent research has shown that his personal campaign of terror, together with his fearsome flagellants, conducted during the Tortosa Disputation, was responsible far more than the Disputation itself for the numbers of Jews converted at this time. A further great influence on the course of events leading to the Expulsion was the book *Fortalitium Fidei* written by Alonso de Espina, a Franciscan. This book, written in 1460, charted in advance the whole pattern of the Spanish Inquisition and the Expulsion of the Jews. It contains strong eschatological elements. It should not be overlooked, also, that there were strong messianic hopes among the Jews too during the 13th, 14th and 15th centuries. It would be an interesting topic of research to trace interconnections during this period between Jewish messianism and Christian apocalypticism. The whole area of Christian apocalypticism in medieval Spain needs further research, though it has already received attention from Margaret Reeves and others.

Thus apocalyptic hopes contributed to the feeling that it was time for a show-down between Christians and Jews, and the era of toleration was drawing to an end. Though the realisation of the importance of the Talmud in Judaism was itself a spur to missionary efforts, because it eroded the false picture of Old Testament Jews on which Augustinian toleration was based, this might not have led to an ultimatum and thus finally to the Expulsion, if a vision of a final solution had not also been strongly present.

Yet a more dominant cause of the Expulsion of the Jews was not so much overt apocalypticism as what might be called the realised apocalypticism of the triumph of the Church. The notion of the Second Coming of Christ was in many official minds submerged in a triumphalism in which the Church was already the fulfilment of eschatological hopes. The Pope as the Vicar of Christ and the Church as the Body of Christ could already be thought of as the earthly manifestation of Christ, making a catastrophic dénouement in terms of the defeat of Antichrist unnecessary. As Christendom, for a period, seemed to be developing towards a unified Papal dominion, it became imperative to purify this mystic body from the contamination of every kind of heresy. On the other hand, the inevitable setbacks experienced to the universalistic aims of the Church produced an anxiety which could only be allayed by intensification of activity against heretics. Since the Jews had been revealed as heretics, being devotees not of the Old Testament but of the Talmud, they could not be tolerated in this new dispensation, and had to be converted or expelled. It might be asked why, in this case, the Jews were not actually exterminated like other heretics, such as the Albigensians. For if the Augustinian basis of toleration had been exploded, what differentiated the Jews from other heretics? The answer may be that the doctrine of Augustine, despite everything, was never totally abandoned. Even if the Jews failed to conform to their Augustinian image, there was still on record an ideal of a "licit" form of Judaism, so that, in its light, existing Jews were imperfect examples of this model, rather than execrable *ab initio*. They could thus be expelled as incorrigible sinners, rather than exterminated as a dangerous heretical threat to the purity of Christian society.

Some questions, however, remain about the connection between the mendicant missionary campaign culminating in the Tortosa Disputation and the eventual expulsion of the Jews from Spain. How was it a solution to expel Jews from one area of Christendom, when they could simply go to another? If the aim was an apocalyptic one, either in the sense of a catastrophic apocalypticism, or a realised apocalypticism, then the only solution would be the expulsion of the Jews from the whole of Christendom. Even this would not be a final solution, since the whole world was to be converted. If, as in fact largely happened, the expelled Jews went to live in Muslim lands, this was only to exacerbate the problem of Islam itself. In fact, we may ask here about the expulsion of the Muslims from Spain, which was scheduled to follow the expulsion of the Jews, though it took over 100 years to accomplish. The Muslims were never protected by an Augustinian-type doctrine, and Islam was regarded as a heresy, not as a "licit" variation of Christianity. Why then were the Muslims given the options of conversion or expulsion, rather than the options of conversion or death like the Albigensians? The answer is that the Muslims were in fact given a starker choice than the Jews when they were threatened with expulsion from Granada and Castile in 1502[4]. The conditions of expulsion were made so unrealistic (for example, they were told that they would have to leave their children behind) that the only viable option was conversion, and the Muslims therefore became converted to Christianity in a body. Their forced conversion, however, was so artificial that they never made any effort to put it into effect, and the task of providing them with a Christian education was so huge that it was abandoned. Consequently, they were eventually expelled (in 1609), but this was an expul-

---

4. Henry Kamen (in Kedourie, 1992, p. 82) has suggested that the reason for this difference was simply that a lesson was learnt from the earlier expulsion of the Jews, which had been a failure in that the main aim, the conversion of the Jews, had not been achieved. Consequently, the Muslims were not given such an opportunity to choose the option of exile. I suggest, on the contrary, that the difference arose from the differing status of Islam, as a heresy, and Judaism, as a licit religion.

sion of Moriscos (i.e. ostensible Christians) not of Muslims as such. The only alternative to the expulsion of the Moriscos would have been to subject them to operations by the Inquisition on an even larger scale than was applied to the Jewish *conversos*.

In any case, Islam was too big a problem to be solved in any radical way. The Crusades had been tried and failed, and the great Islamic world remained to falsify all hopes and predictions of a unified Christian world. Meanwhile, at least part of Christendom could be cleansed of heresy, and this would be an important contribution to an overall solution, for what would God not grant to a Christendom that had shown in at least one of its kingdoms that it could purge its own house. So the Muslims of Spain had to go, and the Jews too could at least be expelled from one holy area of Christendom as an example to the rest. In this way holy Spain led the way towards the achievement of a totally Christian world and the fulfilment of every kind of apocalyptic hope. The Augustinian compromise by which the Jews had been tolerated for a thousand years could still be in force in other areas of Christendom, as long as Spain, triumphant after its conquest of the Muslims, and governed by the Catholic Monarchs, could go beyond that compromise and give a foretaste of the world to come, when heresy and even "licit" Judaism would give way to the universal triumph of Christianity.

The actual reason given officially for the Expulsion of the Jews from Spain had to do with the position of the *conversos*. It was argued that the great numbers of Jews who had been converted could not be expected to remain faithful to Christianity as long as a community of Jews remained to seduce them back to Judaism. But this is not a fully satisfactory explanation of the Expulsion. We have to explain why so many Jews became converted and why their continuing conversion became such a problem. It was the widespread violence against the Jews in 1391 that created a large population of forced converts. Catholic doctrine asserted that though conversion by force was forbidden, once a Jew was converted by force he had to remain Christian, and any attempt to return to Judaism could be investigated and punished by the Inquisition as heresy. What was the impetus that led the Christians of Spain to break the long-established rule against conversion by force? This mass movement of conversion by any and every means was the source of all the troubles of Spanish Jews and also of many serious troubles in Spain itself caused by the crippling expulsions and the resultant neurosis of racialist suspicion of the "New Christians". The infamous record of the Spanish Inquisition (which was set up on lines that were contrary to the wishes of the Papacy) arose directly from the consequences of these forced conversions. There can be little doubt that the impetus to conversion came largely from the activities of the friars, and especially the Dominicans, who organised the Disputations and were prominent in the Inquisition. The massacres and forced conversion of Jews in 1391, the Tortosa Disputation in 1413-4, and the Expulsion itself in 1492, all form part of a single pattern, which is the breakdown of the Augustinian scheme of toleration and the increasingly intense campaign to convert the Jews.

BIBLIOGRAPHY

BAER Yitzhak, *A History of the Jews in Christian Spain*. 2 vols. JPS, Philadelphia, 1971.
COHEN Jeremy, *The Friars and the Jews: the Evolution of Medieval Anti-Judaism*. Cornell University Press, Ithaca, 1982.
MACCOBY Hyam, *Judaism on Trial: Jewish-Christian Disputations in the Middle Ages*. Oxford University Press, London, 1982.
CHAZAN Robert, *Daggers of Faith: Thirteenth Century Christian Missionizing and Jewish Response*. University of California Press, Berkeley, 1989.
CHAZAN Robert, *Barcelona and beyond: the Disputation of 1263 and its Aftermath*. University of California Press, Berkeley, 1992.
KEDOURIE Elie (ed.), *Spain and the Jews*. Thames & Hudson, London, 1992.
PACIOS LOPEZ, A., *La disputa de Tortosa*. 2 vols. Madrid/Barcelona 1957.
REEVES Margaret, *The Influence of Prophecy in the Later Middle Ages: A Study in Joachimism*. Oxford University Press, Oxford, 1969.

Enrique González González

VIVES: UN HUMANISTA JUDEOCONVERSO EN EL EXILIO DE FLANDES [1]

1. El exilio de Joan Lluís Vives (Valencia, 1492/3 - Brujas, 1540) guarda estrecha relación con su origen social judeoconverso. Pero, por sorprendente que parezca, esa circunstancia central de su vida sólo se supo con certeza hace tres décadas. La ignorancia, durante tanto tiempo, de las raíces hebreas del humanista valenciano, no fue casual. Su figura y obra, antes de 1970, apenas si eran conocidas fuera de España. Solía ocupar un lugar secundario entre los fundadores de la pedagogía y la psicología modernas, mérito atribuido en Alemania por los historiadores de la educación en el Renacimiento, a partir de mediados del siglo pasado[2]. Por lo mismo, apenas si se imaginó que su obra tuviese interés más allá de los estrictos campos pedagógico y psicológico.

En España, es cierto, hubo períodos en que el humanista fue mencionado con gran frecuencia, pero solía ocurrir en el marco de discusiones ideológicas que sólo por excepción se tradujeron en auténticos estudios[3]. Para semejantes vivistas, bastaba con sumar el prestigio del nombre a la propia causa. Primero fue reivindicado, a fines del XIX, por los animadores de la Renaixença, que hicieron de él uno de los *precursores* de la entonces llamada *escuela catalana del sentido común*. Llevando más lejos las tesis de los catalanes, Marcelino Menéndez Pelayo (1856-1912) lo declaró *padre* de la filosofía moderna. Don Marcelino, del bando conservador, en polémica con los liberales, que llamaban estéril a la ciencia española y veían el origen de la modernidad en los *extranjeros* Bacon y Descartes, reivindicó la primacía del *español* Vives. Esa *hispanidad* constituyó el único interés para los nacionalistas

---

1. Durante el segundo semestre de 1994, gocé de una estancia de investigación en la Katholieke Universiteit Leuven, invitado por los profesores J. IJsewijn y G. Tournoy. Ahí, el profesor W. Verbeke me invitó a participar en un libro sobre humanismo y exilio, presentando el caso de Vives. En 1987, yo había entregado una nota sobre el tema, en Valencia, que seguía inédita, y decidí reescribirla, ampliándola a más del triple. Por fin, la versión original apareció como "El exilio de Vives, un intelectual judeoconverso del siglo XVI", en M. García (Ed.), *Exiliados. La emigración cultural valenciana a través de los tiempos*, Valencia, Generalitat Valenciana, 1995, 3 vols. Vol. I, pp.11-20. Dedico el presente trabajo a los amigos mencionados y a todos los que contribuyeron a hacer esa recordada estadía tan grata como provechosa.

de extrema derecha de la primera mitad de este siglo, quienes llegaron a imaginar en el valenciano a un precursor del nazismo y al más insigne representante de la *raza* hispana.

Para catalanes y castellanos, pues, Vives importaba en razón de su utilidad como pieza de un discurso nacionalista, de ahí que los pocos que apuntaron la hipótesis de sus orígenes judíos hubiesen sido silenciados o rechazados como aguafiestas. Ya en 1875, Amador de los Ríos

2. Gracias a la publicación del estudio de C. G. Noreña, *Juan Luis Vives*, La Haya, Nijhof, 1970, los lectores de lengua inglesa contaron, por fin, con una monografía moderna y sugerente sobre el valenciano. Su traducción española (Salamanca, Ediciones Paulinas, 1978) contribuyó en mucho a la renovación de la gastada imagen que se tenía de él en la península. La reciente edición crítica de varias obras de Vives y los numerosos estudios aparecidos desde entonces, así sobre él como sobre la escolástica tardía y el humanismo nórdico, han hecho envejecer en importantes aspectos tan meritorio trabajo. La bibliografía posterior ha sido examinada críticamente por V. Del Nero, "Recenti studi su Juan Luis Vives (1970-1985), en *Cultura e Scuola, 102*, (abril-junio, 1987), pp. 121-141; y por A. Monzon, "Bibliografia vivista recent. Balanç y perspectives", en *L'Espill*, 27 (nov. 1987). Una descripción de las ediciones príncipes de Vives, con noticia sobre el grado de avance hacia la edición crítica, E. González, S. Albiñana y V. Gutiérrez (Eds.), *Vives, Edicions prínceps*, Valencia, Generalitat Valenciana-Universitat de València, 1992 (en adelante cito: *Prínceps*, más el n°. de entrada); ver también, G. Tournoy, J. Roegiers y C. Coppens (Eds.), *Vives te Leuven*, Lovaina, Leuven University Press, 1993. El libro de C. G. Noreña, *A Vives bibliography*, Lewinston, N. Y.- Queenston, Ont.- Lampeter, U.K., The Edwin Mellen Press, 1990, contiene, con abundantísimas entradas, notables imprecisiones. Esbocé la recepción de la obra de Vives, en *Joan Lluís Vives, de la escolástica al humanismo*, Valencia, Generalitat Valenciana-Comissió per al V Centenari del descobriment d'America, 1987, cap. II; con mayor detalle, me ocupé de los siglos XVI a XVIII, en un artículo citado, adelante, en nota 79; asimismo, estudié: "La lectura de Vives en los siglos XIX y XX", en J. L. Vives, *Opera omnia*, I, Volumen Introductorio, A. Mestre (Ed.), pp. 1-76, artículo aparecido con varias decenas de erratas. Otros colaboradores del mismo volumen ponen al día la investigación vivista en torno a aspectos particulares de su obra. L. E. Rodríguez-San Pedro Bezares realizó una inteligente aproximación al tema de "Vives: Horizonete de España", en C. Strozetzki (Ed.), *Juan Luis Vives. Sein Werk und seine Bedeutung für Spanien und Deutschland*, Frankfurt am Main, Vervuert, 1995, pp. 186-212; en el mismo volumen, J. F. Alcina, en "Notas sobre la pervivencia de Vives en España (s.XVI)", discutió si la recepción de su obra en la patria fue mayor de lo que normalmente se ha admitido, pp. 213-228.

3. El *Luis Vives y la filosofía del Renacimiento*, de A. Bonilla (Madrid, 1903), fue el trabajo de referencia sobre el humanista durante más de medio siglo, y la única aportación sólida, desde la península, a los estudios vivistas. Bonilla obtuvo noticias, en papeles de la Inquisición, acerca de varios Vives, conversos, en especial de un "Luis Vives, mercader", vivo en 1476, que no pudo identificar con el padre del humanista (cap. I, nota 3), ¿o es que no quiso ir más lejos?

planteó sospechas en ese sentido, sin demasiado eco. Américo Castro, de diversas formas manifestó "que todo en la obra y en la persona de Luis Vives parecía revelar usos exteriores e interiores de la vida hispano-hebraica"[4], y vinculó su exilio en los Países Bajos con dicha circunstancia. La respuesta, si la hubo, fue alegar falta de pruebas. El P. Lorenzo Riber, traductor de Vives al castellano, ilustra bien cuánto irritaba el tema: le merecía "instintiva repulsa" la suposición de "esa mancha ancestral" en "el más cristiano de los epígonos del Renacimiento". Así, a la pregunta por los motivos de su exilio, respondía: "Con espíritu de humildad, confesemos que de todo ello, no sabemos una palabra. Todo ello son puras suspicacias"[5].

Ese fondo ideológico explica la verdadera conmoción que produjo, en 1964, la difusión de los procesos inquisitoriales contra la madre del humanista[6], acusada de judaizar. Urgía un replanteamiento a fondo. Desde entonces se ha reconstruido su genealogía y la macabra actuación de la Inquisición contra la casi totalidad de su familia, con la secuela de muertes y confiscaciones de bienes[7]. Con todo, sigue faltando un esfuerzo análogo para esclarecer lo que tal circunstancia significó en la vida y la obra del exiliado valenciano. Su familia, ¿confesó en secreto la religión mosaica, como pretendía la Inquisición? De ser así, ¿cuál fue el alcance de tales prácticas? ¿Participó en ellas Vives en su niñez, y luego como adulto? Su exilio, ¿fue sólo para ponerse a salvo, o buscaba un mejor clima para judaizar en secreto? ¿Hay evidencias? ¿Es su obra una apología secreta de la vieja ley, o el producto intelectual de un sincero cristiano de origen judeoconverso? Cuestiones válidas, cuyo adecuado planteamiento exige un vasto preámbulo por las discuciones historiográficas que han tenido lugar en torno a la cuestión judeoconversa.

2. Por elemental prudencia, Vives nunca se refirió en público a su origen social converso, aun sabiendo que era un secreto a voces en

---

4. A. Castro, *De la edad conflictiva*, Madrid, Taurus, 1963, 2ª ed., p. 114, entre otros lugares y obras.
5. "Juan Luis Vives, Valenciano", prefacio a la versión castellana de las *Obras Completas*, Madrid, Aguilar, 1947-1948, 2 vols.; vol. I, pp. 15-16 y 25-26.
6. M. de la Pinta LLorente y J. M. de Palacio (Eds.), *Procesos inquisitoriales contra la familia judía de Luis Vives*, Madrid-Barcelona, CSIC, 1964.
7. A. García, *Els Vives: una familia de jueus valencians*, Valencia, Tres y Quatre, 1987; R. García Cárcel, "La familia de Luis Vives y la Inquisición", en *Opera omnia...*, I, Volumen introductorio, pp. 489-519.

España, y sin duda también en la corte de Carlos V. Con todo, en un opúsculo dedicado al inquisidor Manrique, no ocultó críticas medulares al proceder del Santo Oficio. Además, de forma velada pero clara, se refirió ahí mismo al clima de acoso y delación que se vivía en su patria, llamando *exilio* a tan insufrible situación, y *patria* al lugar donde se vivía sin tal suplicio. En otra obra, se manifestó contra la tortura como prueba judicial, y por la educación, antes que la persecución, de los herejes. Esas referencias – que para algunos equivalen a silencio – se complementan con menciones, en cartas privadas, a la rigidez ideológica imperante en España. Tales pasajes, reunidos y puestos en su contexto, ayudan a comprender cómo Vives experimentó su exilio, y su desacuerdo con los métodos del santo tribunal y su secuela de persecuciones como las sufridas por su familia y sus amigos erasmistas en la península.

En el presente trabajo intento, primero, reflexionar en términos generales sobre los enfoques de la historiografía a la cuestión judeoconversa, y señalo que ha predominado la tendencia a asumir, casi tautológicamente, la ecuación: condenado por judaizar = culpable de judaizar. Una perspectiva demasiado sesgada, a mi entender, hacia la vertiente religiosa del problema, y que deja en penumbra los numerosos condicionantes políticos, sociales y jurídicos que intervenían en las resoluciones del tribunal inquisitorial. Me refiero también a quienes, por considerar un tanto acrítica la mencionada visión del problema, han propuesto otras interpretaciones.

A continuación, planteo la cuestión conversa como un fenómeno social de exclusión, por parte de los llamados cristianos *viejos*, contra la casta de los cristianos *nuevos*, orillados a la muerte, al exilio, o a un estatuto de segregación. Y dado que a la base del repudio se alegaba el sedimento judío del grupo marginado, sostengo que los mecanismos de exclusión abarcaron al colectivo en su conjunto, no solamente a quienes judaizaban en secreto. Por ello, dedico especial atención al arma maestra de los intolerantes: el proceso inquisitorial, auténtica maquinaria de víctimas, más allá de la culpa de los procesados, y que llevó a las llamas a comunidades enteras a título de judaizar. Destaco también que muchos contemporáneos no juzgaron la actuación del tribunal como una objetiva y desinteresada búsqueda de la verdad, y alegaron que éste procedía en función de intereses menos puros, con funestas consecuencias. Ello me permite situar a Vives en el marco de esas voces críticas del tribunal y sus secuelas.

En la última parte exploro, en función de las anteriores consideraciones, las circunstancias que orillaron a Vives al exilio, la forma como él cuestionó el procedimiento y los resultados de la Inquisición, y su propuesta de una sociedad armónica, en la que, gracias a la concordia imperante entre sus miembros, ninguno de ellos se veía forzado a buscar nueva patria en tierras ajenas, aunque menos ásperas que la natal.

I. JUDÍOS Y CONVERSOS: UN TERRITORIO POR REPENSAR

Los historiadores ante el problema

3. La historiografía de corte tradicional acerca de los conversos, cuando se escribe desde una perspectiva judía, ha tendido a afirmar, sin cortapisas, que aquéllos, en su *vast majority,* se bautizaron sólo para librarse de la muerte; pero que: *In race, in belief, and largely in practice, they remained as they were before the conversion. They were Jews in all but name, and Christians in nothing but form*[8].

Esa tesis, como se ha puesto de relieve, es compartida, a su modo, por los más conservadores autores católicos. Así, el padre Pinta Llorente, al prologar la edición de los procesos contra la madre de Vives, admite implícitamente el "judaísmo" de los conversos cuando explica a la Inquisición como defensora de "la entraña castiza del alma española" en contraste con el "carácter no nacional que se daba a la raza judía, su proclividad hacia la libertad de pensamiento... desvirtuando los linajes con quienes conviven". Por lo mismo, se trataba de

---

8. C. Roth, *A History of the Marranos*, Londres-Filadelfia, The Jewish Publication Society of America, 1932. Ver especialmente, p. 19. Hay traducción castellana, con el significativo título: *Los judíos secretos. Historia de los marranos* (trad. J. Novella), Madrid, Altalena, 1979. No me propongo censar la vastísima bibliografía sobre el tema. E. Rivkin, en "How Jewish were the New Christians" (*Hispania Judaica* 1 [1980], pp. 101-115), divide a los autores en dos bandos: el "conventional", representado por Roth, H. C. Lea, Y. Baer, H. Kamen, H. Beinart, I. S. Révah, etc., quienes asumen sin mayor problema que los perseguidos por la Inquisición efectivamente judaizaban; y el partido de los que han revisado críticamente, con diverso grado de radicalismo, ese presupuesto: B. Netanyahu – al que citaré adelante –, A. J. Saraiva, y el propio autor, entre otros. Para bibliografía más reciente, casi siempre en la línea tradicional: H. Méchoulan (Ed.), *Les Juifs d'Espagne: histoire d'une diaspora 1492-1992*, Mayenna, Librairie Européenne des idées- Séfarad 92 France (1992); y E. Kedourie (Ed.), *Spain and the Jews. The Sepharadi Experience, 1492 and After*, Londres, Thames and Hudson, 1992. Ambos han sido traducidos en España. Ver también la "Introduction" del presente volumen.

una raza hostil a "los fundamentos dogmáticos en los que España confiaba su pervivencia histórica"[9].

Unos y otros historiadores adoptan perspectivas apologéticas. Los primeros toman el partido de las víctimas; los otros, el de los verdugos. En el campo vivista, A. García asume una posición projudía; Pinta, la inversa. Y con ser tan antagónicos sus puntos de vista, ambos coinciden en algo capital: calificar, sin matiz, de *judía* a la familia de Vives, omitiendo todo análisis de los alcances de tal afirmación[10].

En el extremo opuesto, otros autores han pretendido probar que el alegado judaísmo de los conversos fue una maquinación forjada, a partes más o menos iguales, por los delatores, los jueces, y los propios acusados, sometidos a coacción física y moral para delatar culpas y cómplices reales o imaginarios. Que el tribunal, más que perseguir a judaizantes, los habría fabricado[11].

Menos aprioristas, autores como B. Netanyahu[12], a partir de fuentes hebreas contemporáneas, aportan evidencias insoslayables de que, dentro y fuera de España, los judíos contemporáneos vieron a los conversos como a paganos, debido a la rapidez con que dieron la espalda a la fe ancestral. Tal alejamiento lo documentó ya en torno a la generación de 1391, la víctima de las grandes matanzas y de las consiguientes conversiones masivas de fines del XIV, que trajeron la decadencia o el fin de las aljamas de Sevilla y Valencia, entre otras. Además, sostiene que esas fuentes evidencian, durante el XV, una irreversibe cristianización de los conversos, por lo que, a fin de siglo, apenas si sobrevivirían núcleos aislados de criptojudaísmo, los cuales

> were constantly narrowing in scope and weakening in the intensity of their Jewish devotion, as their practice of Judaism was lim-

---

9. Pinta, *Procesos...*, "Introducción", pp. 11-32.

10. En ambos casos, ya desde los respectivos títulos de sus libros, se aserta ese carácter "judío".

11. El citado E. Rivkin propone que la pregunta misma sobre el presunto judaísmo de los conversos sea considerada un sinsentido, dándole el mismo rango de otras "non-questions" como la de: "Did the Jews commit ritual murder?" (p. 105). I. S. Révah, "Les Marranes", en *Revue des Etudes Juives*, CXVIII (1959-1960), pp. 29-77, califica las tesis de Rivkin y otros autores críticos, de "simplistes ou paradoxales", ver pp. 43-53.

12. *The Marranos of Spain. From the Late XIVth to the Early XVIth Century*, According to contemporary Hebrew Sources, Nueva York, American Academy for Jewish Research, 1966. Un tanto tardía es la versión castellana, revisada por el autor, de C. Morón Arroyo, s. l., Junta de Castilla y León, 1994.

ited to the performance of *certain* Jewish rites only. While crypto-Judaism was thus dwindling, the process of assimilation, both social and religious, was advancing without letup, so much so that when the Inquisition was established... the Marrano camp as a whole appeared to Spain's Jews as a predominantly gentile camp (p. 75).

De lo argumentado, el autor concluyó que, cuando la Inquisición trató a los marranos como a herejes ocultos, "was operating with a fiction", misma que atribuyó a razones políticas y de odio racial, más que a celo religioso (pp. 2-3).

Así, mientras unos historiadores afirman casi sin reserva que los conversos judaizaban, otros optan por la negativa tajante. Entre ambos, un tercer partido ha sostenido una rápida cristianización de los conversos, correlativa a la decadencia experimentada por las comunidades hebreas desde finales del XV. Según ellos, a medida que avanzaba el siglo, el criptojudaísmo era sólo un fenómeno esporádico, ligado confusamente a manifestaciones residuales de la vieja cultura.

Como puede apreciarse, la respuesta de cada autor a la cuestión del presunto judaísmo de los conversos, ha condicionado todo su ulterior tratamiento del problema.

Un deslinde por replantear

4. Tanto los autores que defienden el judaísmo esencial de la *vast majority* de los conversos como quienes afirman su rápida cristianización, suelen admitir la existencia de falsos convertidos, al lado de otros, asimilados de buen grado la nueva religión. Por tal motivo, se ha introducido una distinción que hoy tiende a ser aceptada sin suficiente examen: se aplica el término *converso* o *verdadero converso* a quienes efectivamente cambiaron su fe con el bautismo, y se reserva el de *marrano* para los que siguieron, *in pectore,* fieles a la ley de Moisés, al margen de si volvían a adoptar o no sus prácticas tradicionales.

Hasta donde conozco, la exposición más sugerente de dicha dicotomía, es la de I. S. Révah, en su acreditado artículo "Les Marranes"[13], lleno de fecundas propuestas metodológicas, como ésa fundamental de que conviene estudiar por separado el mundo de los marranos portugueses y el de los castellano-aragoneses; asimismo, es oportuno su lla-

---

13. Ver, arriba, nota 10.

mado a establecer la cronología del problema converso: en ambos asuntos, mucho se ha avanzado desde entonces. Por desgracia, el artículo dice poco acerca de cómo un historiador de los "auténticos" marranos puede deslindar su objeto específico de estudio respecto de dos campos contiguos: el de los "auténticos" conversos, y el de los indecisos o los indiferentes.

En efecto, Révah muestra convincentemente la existencia de individuos bautizados que, no obstante, mantuvieron una *religion marranique*, calificada por él de *Judaïsme potentiel,* pero diversa del judaísmo "par des suppressions et des additions", tales, como la ausencia de circuncisión, de predicación rabínica y de varios ritos, y que, en cambio, creó nuevas plegarias y ceremonias. En consecuencia, "on peut énumérer les attitudes religieuses diverses que les documents historiques nous permettent de reconstituer" (p. 53-56). Para él, los testimonios básicos son los procesos inquisitoriales, leídos con actitud crítica: ni admitiendo literalmente todas sus afirmaciones, ni negándoles de plano validez sólo porque, a veces, como con los supuestos asesinatos rituales, se hubiera incurrido en yerros judiciales.

Menos sustentable parece, en mi opinión, el siguiente paso del autor: "Si l'on accepte notre *definition* du "marranisme" comme un Judaïsme potentiel, *il devient clair que la plupart* des "Nouveaux-Chretiens" poursuivis par les Inquisitions peninsulaires *étaient réelement des judaïsants"* (p. 57, subrayados míos). De la definición formal del objeto de estudio, pasa a la afirmación categórica de su existencia masiva. Tal conclusión *devient claire* para él, exclusivamente en la medida que la está presuponiendo, no demostrando. Él mismo reconoce que no todos los condenados por la Inquisición habrían sido verdaderos judaizantes, al referirse al "pauvre accusé qui meurt sur le bûcher et dont on ne saura sans doute jamais s'il fut vraiment un crypto-juif" (p. 47). Admite, además, la dificultad de ir al fondo: "il s'agit souvent de croyances conservées dans le secret des consciences"(p. 53).

Resulta, en consecuencia, que no es posible desentrañar con certeza, a través de los documentos inquisitoriales, la íntima conciencia de cada procesado. Y a la inversa, que no todos los "verdaderos" marranos habrían sido descubiertos por la Inquisición, de modo que éstos – salvo casos excepcionales – no dejaron trazas útiles para el historiador. De ahí que, el procedimiento ensayado por autores como Révah para escindir el ámbito judeoconverso en dos zonas autónomas, determinadas por su "auténtica" fidelidad a una u otra ortodoxia, no resulte historiográficamente verificable. Por lo mismo, todo estudio del mundo converso basado en semejante distinción se funda en supuestos aprioristicos que, al deslindar arbitrariamente a los integrantes de un colectivo tan problemático, dificultan aún más su comprensión.

Los judaizantes ocultos, los conversos sinceros y los indiferentes o indecisos formaban parte de un mismo conjunto social, dentro del cual un deslinde tajante es imposible, o poco menos. Primero, por lo difícil que resulta al historiador decidir en cuestiones de conciencia; segundo, debido al carácter tan sesgado de la fuente principal para el estudio del colectivo: los procesos inquisitoriales; por último, a causa de que los individuos y grupos sociales no viven estáticamente una creencia, y menos aún en tiempos de conflicto y persecución. Un mismo individuo o comunidad podían asumir diversos credos y actitudes religiosas a lo largo del tiempo, en razón de las circunstancias. Es pues ingenuo e infundado pretender que, en su gran mayoría, los conversos, perseguidos por décadas, y marginados durante siglos, se hubieran mantenido inamoviblemente "judíos" en su fuero interno.

Esa dificultad para determinar la conciencia de los nuevamente bautizados vuelve por tanto improcedente la nomenclatura hoy en uso, que adjudica el mote de "converso" a los *verdaderos* cristianos y reserva el de "marrano" sólo para los judaizantes. Peor aún, porque la distinción no responde a los usos de la época, cuando ambos motes zaherían por igual a los mismos individuos. Así, en 1516, el agente del cardenal Cisneros en la corte de Bruselas indicó al joven rey Carlos quiénes "eran confessos de los questaban aquí", agregando que a todos ellos "los quieren mal"[14]. Meses más tarde, Erasmo expresó el disgusto que le producía esa corte, infestada de *marrani*[15]. No por caso, el aún oscuro humanista Vives era uno de los denostados "confessos" o "marranos" en busca de colocación en el séquito del joven monarca.

Así, cuando los contemporáneos mostraban su antipatía contra los cristianos descendientes de judíos, no establecían distingos sobre las cualidades o defectos de unos u otros individuos del grupo: los descalificaban en cuanto tales y de antemano. Los judíos solían ser mal vistos

---

14. Carta de D. López de Ayala al cardenal, Bruselas, 2. 12. 1516, editada en M. Jiménez Fernández, *Bartolomé de las Casas*, vol. I, Sevilla, C. S. I. C.-E. E. H. A., 1953, pp. 535-40.

15. Erasmo a W. Pirckheimer, 2. 11. 1517, en P. S. Allen, H. M. Allen, y H. W. Garrod (Eds.), *Opus epistolarum D. Erasmi Roterodami*, Oxford, 1906-1957, 12 vols; vol. III, ep. 694.

por los cristianos, pero, con anterioridad a 1492, la ley garantizaba la práctica de su religión y de sus usos sociales. En cambio, los conversos, dado que procedían de la ley mosaica, eran todos, al menos, sospechosos de conservarla en su fuero interno y de urdir maquinaciones perversas contra sus nuevos correligionarios. A su vez, y este dato fundamental no siempre se tiene en cuenta, el hecho de que todos fuesen bautizados, los ponía bajo la jurisdicción y a merced de la comunidad cristiana tradicional, y dominante.

Es a la luz de ese complejo conflicto social entre dos colectivos, el de los cristianos "viejos", en su conjunto, contra los "nuevos", como se puede intentar comprender el dramático fenómeno de los conversos. Reducirlo a la cuestión de qué tan judíos eran en su interior los descendientes de los nuevos bautizados, es limitarse a una sola de sus manifestaciones, la menos factible de fundamentar historiográficamente.

5. Al margen de las mencionadas objeciones, numerosos autores, una vez prejuzgada la "esencial" o "potencial" condición judía de la *vast majority* de la comunidad conversa, tienden a estudiarla como a mera parcela de la historia del pueblo elegido. Así, su interés se limita, bien a aquel sector de la población acusada de judaizar – inculpación que, al igual que los inquisidores, se apresuran a dar por buena –, o también, al de quienes recobraron sus raíces religiosas, perpetuándose en nuevas comunidades sefarditas fuera de la patria. De ahí la atención que ha merecido la diáspora portuguesa[16]. En cambio, poco sabemos de

16. Durante mucho tiempo – y todavía en la actualidad autores como Kedourie, en el prefacio a su volumen – se ha tendido a asimilar el fenómeno de los judeoconversos castellanos y aragoneses con el de los portugueses, sin tener en cuenta las circunstancias tan específicas vividas por los hebreos en el último reino, y que ya Révah realzara oportunamente. A diferencia de Castilla y Aragón, las conversiones masivas de judíos portugueses no tuvieron lugar hasta 1497, al dárseles la disyuntiva del bautismo o el exilio. Ya bautizados, la situación de sus comunidades sólo se vio seriamente amenazada a partir de 1537, al implantarse la Inquisición. De ahí la relativa facilidad con que los bautizados volvieron a la antigua fe y reconstituyeron su vida tradicional, primero en Portugal y luego en el exilio. En ese marco, resultan explicables casos como los de los dos humanistas portugueses analizados en el presente volumen por H. Tucker, quien muestra cómo Didacus Pyrrus Lusitanus, al igual que Amatus Lusitanus, se expresaron simultáneamente como humanistas cristianos y como autores hebreos. Por tales peculiaridades, cada vez más autores, como Révah y A. Novinsky, han comprendido la conveniencia metodológica de deslindar sistemáticamente el ámbito portugués del castellanoaragonés. Para una visión de conjunto, con la bibliografía básica, A. Novinsky, "Juifs et Noveaux chrétiens du Portugal", en H. Méchoulan (Ed.), *Les Juifs d'Espagne...*, pp. 73-107.

la suerte de otros conversos, valencianos, andaluces y, sin duda de otras regiones que, huyendo del peligro, se asentaron en Flandes a fines del XV y principios del XVI, los cuales, hasta donde hay indicios, murieron con fama de cristianos, asimilados a la sociedad que les dio refugio, pero guardando ciertos rasgos comunes y formas de solidaridad.

Si el caso de Vives resulta ilustrativo, es posible advertir, por noticias aisladas, que ya desde su primer viaje a Brujas, hacia 1512, tuvo buena acogida en el seno de esa comunidad, a la que lo unían lazos de parentesco, y dentro de la cual se casó. Hay asimismo indicios de que, al enviudar quien sólo después sería su suegra, Vives veló por su patrimonio familiar, y consta documentalmente que cuidó de la educación, la colocación y los intereses de sus cuñados. Tales conversos – la falta de estudios impide saber por cuántas generaciones – aparte de su tradicional aplicación a tareas urbanas como el comercio o profesiones liberales como la medicina, habrían guardado hábitos alimenticios propios – a los que Vives se dijo aficionado alguna vez – y, sin duda, otras formas de convivencia y de solidaridad[17]. Es un territorio que espera ser esclarecido.

II. LOS MECANISMOS DE LA EXCLUSION

Un conflicto de "naciones"

6. Los orígenes del problema judeoconverso son bastante conocidos y aceptados por la mayoría de los autores, para que necesite demorarme en este punto. Se ha señalado que, a fines de la edad media, entró en crisis irreversible la ambivalente tolerancia de la *nación* cristiana de Castilla y Aragón para con la judía, hasta volverse intransigencia.

Dependientes directos de la jurisdicción real, los hebreos peninsulares obtuvieron de los sucesivos monarcas privilegios varios que garantizaban sus prácticas religiosas, usos sociales y actividades económicas, de carácter principalmente urbano. En numerosas ciudades, ese estilo de vida tomó forma jurídica en la aljama, suerte de ayuntamiento sin territorio propio, pero que proveía el culto religioso, la educación literaria, la justicia, y los tributos y servicios económicos al rey. Tal normativa era, en parte, consecuencia de la marginación ejercida por la

---

17. Ver *Joan Lluís Vives...*, cap. III.

sociedad cristiana, pero también la exigían los usos de solidaridad, de higiene, alimenticios, etc.[18], de la comunidad hebrea.

Los motivos de esa acentuada intolerancia, y las razones por las que se perpetuó hasta el fin del antiguo régimen, han sido objeto de largas discusiones, que llegan hasta hoy. Guardaron incuestionable relación con la serie de crisis económicas, mortandades, conflictos políticos y luchas civiles ocurridos a lo largo del siglo XIV, y sufridos por Castilla y Aragón, en cada reino a su modo. Cupo una parte además, al aumento de la presión política contra los judíos, fomentada por el celo proselitista de predicadores frailes, como Vicent Ferrer, o seculares, como aquel arcediano de Écija, cuyos arrebatos habrían inducido la masacre de 1391, en Sevilla. Una explosión que contagiaría a las principales ciudades de las dos coronas. Asimismo, se fue consolidando el afán de los monarcas por imponer su cetro sobre la sociedad en su conjunto, con creciente rechazo a tolerar diferencias y excepciones[19].

Más allá de la importancia que cada autor concede a los pogromos de 1391, existe acuerdo en que se trata de una fecha emblemática, de no retorno. Por los motines se arruinaron, si no desaparecieron, las aljamas de Sevilla, Segovia, Barcelona o Valencia. Muchos supervivientes fueron forzados al bautismo o a buscar seguridad en pequeñas ciudades. Desaparecieron o decayeron las condiciones para una cabal práctica de los usos sociales y religiosos, menguando la instrucción literaria y la predicación rabínica. Durante las décadas siguientes, gran número de esos judíos se convirtieron por la presión de una legislación intolerante e intolerable, por las prédicas, o por creer que su situación mejoraría con la nueva ley. Los propios historiadores hebreos han insistido en la acusada indiferencia religiosa de las capas altas de la población judía antes mismo de las persecuciones, lo que facilitaría, en condiciones adversas para la fe ancestral, la conversión.

Durante las primeras décadas, el proceso de fusión de los conversos con la casta dominante se dio sin notables conflictos, y sin que faltara

---

18. El clásico estudio de Y. Baer, en su versión castellana, *Historia de los judíos en la España cristiana,* trad. del hebreo por J.L. Lacave, Barcelona, Altalena, 1981, 2 vols., ofrece una bibliografía actualizada.

19. Con todo, autores como H. Kamen creen que insistir en el factor del absolutismo monárquico, es mero resabio de la historiografía decimonónica, más que hecho histórico comprobado. Ver su colaboración en el volumen editado por E. Kedourie, *Spain and the Jews...* Sin embargo, documentos como el que cito el la siguiente nota, parecen avalar la tesis de la creciente intransigencia real.

cierto cinismo en una parte de los neófitos para mantener o adaptar viejas prácticas. La alta nobleza no parece haberse inquietado por los recién llegados, a diferencia de las oligarquías urbanas, recelosas de la competencia de los nuevos, y de las capas medias y bajas de las ciudades, para no hablar de los campesinos, que transladaron a los conversos su antipatía tradicional para con los hebreos. Se alzaron unas voces en favor de la cabal integración de los confesos, y de darles instrucción religiosa, pero pronto ganaron los *duros*. La irrupción de los Reyes Católicos, el último cuarto del siglo XV, volcó la balanza en favor de los "viejos" cristianos, impulsores de medidas que acarrearían la persistente marginación de la nueva casta, con la ruina económica y la eliminación física de muchos de sus miembros.

De una parte, estaba el interés de los católicos monarcas por imponer orden, tras décadas de conflictos políticos y guerras civiles, con su cauda de transtornos sociales que, a su vez, contribuían a acentuar la hostilidad contra los conversos. Para arreglar el innegable embrollo religioso[20], en 1480 la corona ensayó la separación drástica de los judíos, mandándoles vivir en barrios cercados por muros. Cuando juzgó ineficaz ese aislamiento interno, decretó su definitiva expulsión de los reinos. Entre tanto, para corregir a los conversos que judaizaban, los reyes introdujeron el tribunal inquisitorial en Castilla, poniéndolo bajo sus órdenes y, poco después, suplantaron en Aragón la vieja Inquisición papal con la de nuevo cuño. Para los monarcas – como veremos –, la eficacia de la nueva institución derivaba precisamente de su rigor, y al frente de ella pusieron, durante los primeros y decisivos años, a funcionarios llenos de celo anticonverso que al punto activaron una poderosa maquinaria de terror. Éste, lejos de constituir una desviación,

---

20. J. A. Llorente citó un documento (hoy, Inq., lib. 572, Archivo Historico Nacional, Madrid – en adelante: AHN-M) sobre una junta de consejeros reales en el recién conquistado reino de Granada, en 1499: "Después de muchas conferencias vinieron a conformarse en que *todo el mal provenía de la diversidad de religiones* y que no tendría remedio eficaz mientras no fuesen cristianos todos los habitantes; por lo cual era forzoso procurar la conversión de los moros y fijar en Granada inquisición contra los cristianos nuevos" (*Anales de la Inquisición en España*, I, Madrid, 1812, p. 255. Cit. por J. Meseguer Fernández, "Fernando de Talavera, Cisneros y la Inquisición en Granada", en J. Pérez Villanueva (Ed.), *La Inquisición española. Nueva visión, Nuevos horizontes,* Madrid, S. XXI, 1980, pp. 371-400; p.372). Aunque referida a los moros – la otra gran minoría, que aquí no tocaré –, la cita ilustra meridianamente la nueva mentalidad imperante.

era uno de los fines del tribunal: disuadir por miedo al castigo. Antes que punible, era un rigor ejemplar. De ahí el boato de los autos de fe[21].

Montado el aparato inquisitorial como instrumento monárquico de una política religiosa, los enemigos de los conversos, por su parte, vieron en aquél un formidable instrumento judicial para expresar su odio contra la *generación* y vengar agravios reales o supuestos, particulares o colectivos. Intolerancia contra la *nación* judía y judeoconversa que rayó en actitudes sin duda racistas – bien documentadas por Méchoulan a partir de la segunda mitad del siglo XVI[22] –, pero que envolvía un problema más complejo. Como se sabe, en una sociedad de castas se tiene por buen orden aquél en el que cada una se contiene en los límites de su estamento, sin rebasarlo hacia arriba ni abajarse. En tanto que *nación* o casta aparte, se juzgaba propio de los judíos que se ocuparan en "tratos de mercaderías", "cambios" y "otros oficios mecánicos y viles", actividades vistas como improcedentes para hidalgos, gente "honrada" y labradores[23].

Ahora bien, cuando los cristianos forzaron a los judíos a bautizarse, el sacramento desató las ataduras que, por tradición, contenían a Israel dentro de su casta, abriéndole espacios antes intransitables: la compra de tierras, vedada desde el siglo XIII, los matrimonios ventajosos, la colocación en cabildos civiles y eclesiásticos, los altos cargos en órdenes religiosas, y hasta algunos obispados, como el de Burgos para los Santamaría, el padre y luego el hijo, o Granada, concedido a fray Hernando de Talavera. Con todo, los conversos, al invadir *sus* altos espa-

---

21. Sobre el inabarcable tema de la Inquisición, ver la *Bibliotheca Bibliographica Historiae Sanctae Inquisitionis,* de E. van der Vekene, Vaduz, 1982-1983, 2 vols. Con importantes documentos, J. A. Llorente, *Historia crítica de la Inquisición en España*, Madrid, Hiperión, 1981, 4 vols. Insustituible, el estudio de H. C. Lea, que en su versión castellana, por A. Alcalá, restituye a la lengua original los textos traducidos por el autor, y actualiza la signatura de los documentos citados: *Historia de la Inquisición española*, Madrid, FUE, 1983, 3 vols. Útiles, los manuales de B. Benassar, *L'Inquisition espagnole XVe- XIXe siècle*, Évreux, Hachette, 1979; y H. Kamen, *Inquisition and Society in Spain,* Londres, Weidenfeld and Nicolson, 1985; ambos traducidos al castellano. De J. Pérez, hay un reciente resumen sobre la: *Historia de una tragedia. La expulsión de los judíos de España*, Barcelona, Crítica, 1993.

22. "L'alterité juive dans la pensée espagnole (1550-1650)", en *Studia Rosenthaliana,* vol. VIII, 1(1974), pp. 31-58; y 2 (1974), pp. 171-204.

23. Cuando se averiguó la limpieza de sangre del futuro cardenal e inquisidor general, Diego de Espinosa, en 1566, se concluyó que sus modestos parientes "siempre han vivido como hijosdalgos onrada y principalmente, y que nunca tuvieron *tratos de mercaderías ni cambios ni otros oficios mecánicos ni viles*" AHN-M, Órdenes Militares, exp. 2758: cit. en J. Martínez Millán (Dir), *La corte de Felipe II,* Madrid, Alianza Universidad, 1994, p. 198. Un ejemplo entre miles.

cios a los cristianos viejos, no por ello abandonaron las profesiones "bajas", identificadas por el pueblo con la detestada casta hebrea: siguieron dedicándose también a contadores reales y de nobles, a corredores, comerciantes, recaudadores y arrendadores de impuestos, prestamistas, etc. Es verdad que los más pobres del grupo seguían limitados, como antes de la conversión, al ámbito de las tareas manuales. Si esa doble conducta – seguir viviendo "como judíos" pero invadiendo sus tradicionales espacios a la nobleza, a las ciudades y a la iglesia – se toleraba en tiempos de paz y buenas cosechas, la escasez y los desórdenes desataban la ira popular anticonversa[24].

De ese modo, la política de los Reyes Católicos para poner orden en los medios judíos y conversos confluyó, por razones de diverso orden, con la tradicional inquina popular contra la otra casta. La convergencia de ese odio social con las medidas políticas de la corona, hizo de la Inquisición un instrumento que fue mucho más lejos de su finalidad original: no sólo perseguiría y castigaría a los judaizantes sino, de forma activa o pasiva, a los descendientes de linaje de hebreos, judaizaran o no[25].

El decisivo aporte popular a la tarea punitiva de la Inquisición real tuvo su expresión, como veremos, a través de los numerosos funcionarios del tribunal de baja extracción social cristianovieja, y mediante la fundamental tarea de los delatores. En documentos de crítica al tribunal solía insistirse en los daños que acarreaba poner a éste en manos, no de "ydalgos", sino de "labradores, porque cossa rrecia es que labradores sean jueces de conversos, porque son ynimicíssimos". Asimismo, se cuestionaba la aceptación de calumnias contra la persona mejor afa-

---

24. El cronista de los Reyes Católicos, A. Bernáldez, cura de los Palacios, ilustra bien esa ambivalencia recelosa del pueblo bajo contra los conversos. Ver *Historia de los Reyes Católicos*, en *Crónicas de los Reyes de Castilla (III)*, Biblioteca de Autores Españoles, LXX, Madrid, Atlas, 1953; cap. 43. J. Pérez, en *Historia de una tragedia...*, insiste, acertadamente, en que la intolerancia popular solía exacerbarse en tiempos de desorden y escasez de pan.

25. Resulta significativo que, incluso en un libro tan renovador como el citado de B. Benassar, al tratar de "La répression des minorités", se hable de "Les offensives contre *les juifs et les crypto-judaïsants*" (p. 138), implicando, tal vez por inadvertencia, que la actividad anticonversa alcanzaba sólo a infractores. A menos que se admita que todo cristiano nuevo, en tanto que procesado, judaizaba. Es verdad que pronto el tribunal extendió su jurisdicción a otros campos, pero los documentos reales y pontificios de erección, y las primeras *Instrucciones* para los funcionarios, apenas si previeron otro objetivo que los conversos.

mada, obra de "la triste mugercilla y el pobre rústico y qualquier lego que allí [en el tribunal] entra"[26].

Un aspecto en modo alguno secundario de la persecución contra los conversos, consistió en el asalto a sus bienes. No sólo mediante los ocasionales saqueos cuando estallaba la ira popular. También, a través de la sistemática requisa de sus bienes por parte del tribunal, que llevó a la ruina a los miembros más conspicuos de esta comunidad y a gran número de los medianamente acomodados, como los Vives. En efecto, a más de la infamia que recaía sobre los inculpados y su familia, excluyéndolos por generaciones de los más importantes oficios y dignidades, se los privaba de sus bienes. De ellos se sustentó – hasta bien entrado el siglo XVI – el tribunal, y servían para premiar a funcionarios diligentes y a denunciadores de bienes escondidos. Descontado lo anterior – si los jueces se esmeraban en sus secuestros y los administraban con parsimonia –, el resto pasaba a las arcas del rey[27].

Esa "persecución económica" de los conversos se volvía, pues, indispensable para la existencia misma del aparato inquisitorial. En la medida que los gastos del tribunal, los costes del proceso y de los alimentos de los presos iban por cuenta de las víctimas, es evidente que, si la persecución se hubiera dirigido sólo o principalmente contra los conversos pobres, la insolvencia de éstos habría acarreado la quiebra del Santo Oficio. A la inversa, a mayores fortunas golpeadas, más seguros tendrían los funcionarios su pan y el beneplácito del rey, a cuyo fisco iban los excedentes. De ahí la innegable selectividad de la persecución, que amenazaba en mayor medida a los conversos ricos. Al

---

26. En el memorial anónimo de un clérigo de Toledo contra los procedimientos de la Inquisición, de 1538, al que dedicaré un apartado más adelante, § 9, aparecen tales conceptos: AHN-M, Inq., lib. 1325, h. 17 y 18.

27. De hecho, ya las Instrucciones dadas por Torquemada en 1484, y las del año siguiente (editadas por Lea, v. I, pp. 827-835), son un auténtico manual de secuestros de bienes. En carta a Torquemada, de 22 de julio de 1486, Fernando el Católico protestaba de tantos gastos, y le pedía moderación, "porque se así no lo fazen, más montarán los salarios que [no lo que] proceda de la Inquisición" Lea, I, p. 822. R. García Cárcel, en *Orígenes de la Inquisición española. El tribunal de Valencia*, Barcelona, Península, 1976, estudió las cuentas del tribunal valenciano de 1476 a 1530; totalizó como ingresos (para los 31 años de que existen datos) 6,431,517 sueldos, mientras que, como egresos (para los 34 años conocidos), sólo 3,476,085 sueldos, pp. 34-37. El saldo a favor, casi la mitad, pasaba al fisco real, a razón de poco menos de 100.000 anuales. Como mero indicador del alcance de esas sumas, menciono que, en 1491, la dote de la madre de Vives, quien procedía de una familia acomodada, montó 10,000 sueldos.

menos eso señaló al rey un memorialista, en 1538: "el que más hávil es en ganar haçienda, esos tienen el mayor peligro, y essos son los que no se escapa ninguno deste laço; *en especial los conversos, que no escapa ninguno*"[28]. No es gratuito que, en una carta escrita a raíz de la detención de su padre, Vives hubiera calificado al proceso de "grandísimo y odiosísimo pleito de bienes"[29].

La circunstancia de que en tales conflictos se insinúe una pugna de los elementos más tradicionales de la sociedad – por lo general identificados con los cristianos viejos – en contra de judíos y conversos – urbanos y comúnmente dados a profesiones más activas en lo económico – ha llevado a algunos historiadores a plantear si se trató de una pugna de los sectores "feudales" contra la incipiente burguesía. Sin embargo, no todos los "burgueses" procedían de la casta judaica. Más aún, el mejor conocimiento de aquella economía ha permitido establecer que nunca los judíos o los conversos tuvieron predominio en los campos arquetípicamente asociados a ellos. En todos esos ramos pesó siempre más, cuantitativamente hablando, la actividad económica de los cristianos viejos[30]. Es en cambio innegable que las principales fortunas de los miembros del grupo fueron arrebatadas por la Inquisición, quedando aquél, como tal, empobrecido, y social y jurídicamente marginado. En el mejor de los casos, quienes tenían recursos y suerte, lograban huir del reino. Nicolás Valldaura, futuro suegro de Vives, escapó a Brujas, donde rehizo su hacienda, mientras en Valencia era quemado en efigie[31].

Sin pretender negar la existencia de judaizantes, un examen sucinto de los actores del proceso inquisitorial y de sus características jurídicas permitirá ver la medida en que daba pábulo a la persecución indiscriminada de los conversos, y por qué motivos sus procedimientos fueron cuestionados por contemporáneos como Vives.

28. AHN-M, Inq. lib. 1325, h. 16.

29. H. de Vocht (ed), *Literae virorum eruditorum ad Franciscum Craneveldium (1522-1528)*, Lovaina, 1928; Ep. 32, p. 86-87. Su padre estaba sufriendo, *in bonis etiam maximmam et odiosissimam litem.*

30. A. MacKay, y J. Pérez, entre otros, han insistido en este punto.

31. Si no se trata de un homónimo, en el Archivo del Antiguo Reino de Valencia (En adelante: AARV), Valencia, Mestre Racional, 8346, una nota de febrero de 1500, menciona al futuro suegro de Vives y al padre de aquél, también condenado: "Casa de Nicolás Valldaura, mercader, fijo de Gabriel Valldaura quondam, condepnado; condenado en estatua y relajado. No se hallaron bienes, pero su padre era rico, y se hace el presente".

De la delación a la confesión: el "aparejo" del proceso

7. Independientemente de la gravedad de la falta en que incurriese un acusado, o de su inocencia, todos los críticos contemporáneos del Santo Oficio insistieron en un punto capital de su ejercicio: dejaba prácticamente inerme al detenido frente a unos jueces y unos testigos de excepcional poder.

Estudiosos actuales del carácter jurídico del tribunal, han destacado que su actuación se ajustaba al derecho común en tanto que el crimen de herejía era asimilado al de lesa majestad[32], circunstancia que determinó el carácter de los métodos inquisitoriales. Su práctica judicial no fue, pues, invención "perversa" de la monarquía española: su doctrina jurídica enraizaba en el derecho imperial y en el canónico, y se hallaba plenamente desarrollada en el momento en que los Reyes Católicos la adoptaron para Castilla y Aragón. Nicolás Eymeric, el famoso autor del *Directorium inquisitorum,* escribió ese fundamental prontuario en 1376, es decir, para la Inquisición pontificia. La novedad derivaría de que el papa aceptó poner tan formidable arma en manos de los monarcas hispanos, que supieron transformarla en instrumento de Estado, bajo el nombre de Consejo de la Suprema Inquisición.

Por su carácter de lesa majestad divina, el crimen de herejía era visto "como una excepción al procedimiento ordinario y al procedimiento criminal"[33]. Su peculiaridad se justificaba por lo grave del delito: un delito público que ofendía al pueblo de dios; en consecuencia, todos tenían obligación de delatarlo, so pena de encubrimiento; nunca prescribía: ni con la sentencia, siempre susceptible de revisión, ni con la muerte del delincuente. De ahí la instrucción de procesos como el fallado contra la madre de Vives, veintiún años después de su fallecimiento. Su castigo era la muerte, con pérdida de bienes, y la infamia.

---

32. *Haeresis crimen aequiparatur crimine laesae maiestatis immo, crimen haeresis est gravius*, B. Como, *Lucerna inquisitorum hereticae pravitatis*, Milán, 1566, p. 31, citado en V. Pinto, "Sobre el delito de herejía (siglos XIII-XVI)", en J. A. Escudero (Ed.), *Perfiles jurídicos de la Inquisición española*, Madrid, Instituto de Historia de la Inquisición-Universidad Complutense, 1989, pp. 195-204. En el mismo volumen, de gran interés: E. Gacto, "Aproximación al Derecho penal de la Inquisición", pp. 175-193; así como, A. Pérez Martín, "La doctrina jurídica y el proceso inquisitorial", pp. 279-322.

33. Pérez Martín, cit. en nota anterior, p. 285; el autor hace un examen de notable claridad y rigurosamente justificado, de la doctrina subyacente al proceso, omitiendo, a fuer de buen jurista, toda referencia a posibles manipulaciones de la doctrina durante la práctica procesal.

En consecuencia, el proceso para juzgar la herejía tenía carácter sumario[34], lo que autorizaba a reducir al mínimo los requisitos formales del juicio ordinario, sin por ello invalidarse. Además de sumarios, eran procesos arbitrarios en tanto que la discrecionalidad – el arbitrio – del inquisidor era el criterio último para juzgar a un inculpado. Éste, por su parte, debía defenderse de cargos que ignoraría a lo largo de todo el proceso, y sin otra ayuda que un letrado impuesto por el tribunal. Cargos que eran formulados por delatores cuyo anonimato garantizaba la Inquisición. No se presumía inocencia, sino culpa, misma que el reo debía confesar.

A pesar de la gravedad imputada a la falta, y del rigor excepcional de los procedimientos y los castigos, el delito de herejía no estaba delimitado con nitidez[35], ni bajo qué condiciones se incurría en él. Suárez lo definió como *voluntarius et pertinax error, in materia fidei catholica contraria, in homine, qui se christianum esse profitetur*[36]. Para ser hereje se necesitaba, pues, el bautismo, incurrir en error de fe y, sobre todo, obstinarse en él. La caracterización no podía ser más amplia y maleable. Dicho sea de paso, ningún judío o pagano era susceptible de semejante juicio por un tribunal cristiano: el bautismo era su precondición. Por su parte, la obstinación en el error implicaba un acto voluntario, pero como la voluntad es invisible, sólo se la percibía mediante indicios externos. Éstos podían ser nimios en sí mismos, pero no tanto, si se tomaban como signos de una voluntad perversa. Sólo el arbitrio del inquisidor – y de ahí el carácter arbitrario del juicio – establecía cuál o cuáles de los indicios implicaban herejía. Un autor anónimo expuso al futuro Carlos V, en 1516, que los inquisidores "eran como dioses en la tierra, que hacían lo que querían, porque no había quien les fuese a la mano, ni osase"[37].

---

34. Según una decretal de Bonifacio VIII, citada extensamente por Pérez Martín, p. 281, el juicio debía realizarse *simpliciter et de plano, sine strepitu et figura judicii*. Por su parte, Torquemeda ordenó, en el nº 6 de sus Instrucciones de 1500: *que los inquisidores non consientan dilación en los procesos é procedan sumariamente según la forma del derecho que en este caso de la herejía habla*. Ed. por Lea, I, p. 837.

35. En el tratado anónimo, *Del regimiento de príncipes*, presentado en 1516 al futuro Carlos V, se solicitaba, como quinta cuestión en torno al tribunal: *saber quién es herege, para que se sepa a quién se ha de condenar; porque muchos inquisidores, aunque han condenado a muchos por hereges, no lo saben [...]*, LLorente, *Historia crítica...*, Apénd. X, vol. V, p. 308.

36. V. Pinto, ob. cit., cuya argumentación sigo aquí.

37. Llorente, *Historia crítica...*, IV, p. 300. Que si alguien se atrevía a denunciar a un inquisidor – proseguía el tratadista –, al no existir otra instancia, "eran sus jueces los [=aquellos mismos] de quien había dicho que no guiaban los negocios [...] conforme a derecho".

El nombre de inquisidores dado a tales jueces procedía de su función indagatoria. Debían "recorrer todos los lugares e villas de sus diócesis é partidos", para que "hagan é resciban los testigos"[38]. A partir de tales denuncias, y con la ayuda casuística de los manuales, instruían sus procesos. La *diffamatio*, pues, era el obligado punto de arranque. De ahí que registraran cualquier clase de delaciones, ante todo, la autoinculpación de los propios conversos, que acudían durante el período de gracia, con esperanza de mejor suerte, y entonces se les obligaba a delatar a terceros. El resto de la población era amenazada con excomunión y otras penas si encubría herejes, y se le recitaba una lista de conductas punibles, con algunos signos externos para detectarlas, como el aseo semanal, la compra de lechugas en tiempo de pascua de los ázimos, etc. Por tratarse de procesos sumarios se aceptaba, *in favorem fidei*, a toda clase de testigos[39], aun los que la justicia ordinaria consideraba inválidos, como "los proscritos, perjuros y criminales". El testimonio de los parientes contaba para cargo, pero no para descargo. Si un delator, repreguntado o sometido a tortura, se contradecía, el inquisidor no invalidaba el testimonio inicial: decidía cuál de los dos asertos dar por bueno.

Ciertamente, no todos los delatores tenían la misma calidad. Mientras que dos testigos de los considerados idóneos por la justicia ordinaria valían como prueba plena, si sus deposiciones coincidían, las deposiciones de los restantes acusadores valían como prueba parcial o como indicio.

Los indicios tenían importancia capital en tanto que permitían acusar a cualquier denunciado de *suspectus haeresis*, e incoarle proceso para comprobar un delito ya implícito en la noción de "sospecha": la presunción de un mal a través de sus signos externos. De ahí que el inquisidor no sólo debiera castigar a los legítimos herejes, sino a quien "por sus dichos o actos hay convicción de que es hereje, aun si en hecho de verdad no lo sea"[40]. Esto explica, en buena medida, la

---

38. Instrucciones de Sevilla, 1500, en Lea, vol. I, p. 836.

39. Sobre el carácter de los testigos y el valor de sus denuncias, Pérez Martín, ob. cit., pp. 292-295, y 306-310.

40. Tan importante observación, en al artículo citado de V. Pinto, en especial, pp. 203-204. Cita nada menos que a Domingo Báñez, *De fide, spe et charitate*..., Salamanca, 1568, p. 638: *At vero inquisitores hereticae pravitatis procedunt ex praesumptione, et teneunt punire ut haereticum eum qui ex dictis vel factis convincitur esse haereticus, etiam si non sit re vera haereticus.*

extrema susceptibilidad de los españoles del antiguo régimen ante la fama: la difamación, en tanto que signo externo de algo interior, era ya un principio de delito. Bastaba con que el inquisidor lo demostrara de forma "plena" o "semiplena" para la ruina del sujeto y de su casa.

Cuando el tribunal creía contar con suficientes indicios en contra de alguien, lo llamaba a confesar un delito de herejía que no le era especificado. Todos los subsecuentes mecanismos se encaminaban a lograr su confesión. Si titubeaba, era indicio en su contra; más aún, si se contradecía. Si negaba ser culpable, se le detenía, y sus bienes se confiscaban precautoriamente. A continuación, el reo podía ser coaccionado con promesas, amenazas, con la posposición *sine die* del juicio, aislado de parientes, de amigos y sin confesor ni sacramentos, o también a través del tormento. Si resistía todos esos recursos, negándose a confesar, se aplicaban en su contra todas las pruebas plenas, semiplenas o indicios vehementes aportados por los testigos o por él mismo durante el proceso. La confesión, una vez arrancada, era tenida por prueba plena. Si al otro día de la tortura, el reo se retractaba, se le volvía a someter a la prueba del tormento. Si acababa por admitir un delito en verdad no cometido, su mentira justificaba el que sufriera una pena correspondiente a la culpa confesada... En suma: si el detenido reconocía el crimen imputado, lo hubiese en verdad cometido o no, el inquisidor dictaba la pena correspondiente; si no lo admitía, las delaciones en su contra eran valoradas por el inquisidor, quien dictaba la pena correspondiente.

En cuanto a la defensa, el indiciado debía aceptar a la persona que le designaran, sin posibilidad de letrado propio, ni ayuda de parientes o de amigos. Solía dar una lista de enemigos, para ver si entre ellos estaban los delatores, y también los nombres de personas que, no siendo parientes, pudieran abonar su conducta y, de entre ellos, el juez citaba a quienes tenía a bien. Mientras el preso hablaba con el abogado, debía hacerlo ante los inquisidores, y el notario tomaba la conversación. Si el abogado se convencía de la culpa del cliente, tenía que renunciar a su defensa, e intentar convencerlo de confesar. Por lo demás, al no aplicarse el principio de "cosa juzgada", el reo podía volver a ser procesado o recibir ampliaciones o reducciones de la pena.

Por todo ello, el mencionado clérigo toledano exclamó en el memorial enviado a Carlos V en 1538: "tentar a Dios es querer que, en cada preso por la ynquisición, haga Dios un misterio [=milagro] para que se salve, que por misterio se puede contar el que sale libre, según la poca defenssa tienen, e las rigurosas leyes con que son juzgados" (h.14 v°). Más allá de la amarga ironía, Benassar ha encontrado que, si apremiaba la proximidad de un auto de fe, hasta 42 reos eran despachados en una sola sentencia (p. 34). Por su parte, García Cárcel documentó el procesamiento de 2354 individuos en el tribunal valenciano entre 1484 y 1530. El 91% por ciento de ellos, bajo acusación de judaizar. Se conocen 1997 sentencias de las falladas contra conversos: 909 (el 45%) fueron quemados, en cuerpo o en efigie, lo que valía lo mismo a efectos de pérdida de bienes; 1076 fueron penitenciados con multas de varia magnitud, y únicamente hubo 12 (el 0.6%) absueltos[41]. Aunque los autos de fe no tenían periodicidad fija, la media anual de enviados en Valencia a la hoguera durante el periodo, fue de 19.7.

Si, a pesar de todas esas singularidades procesales, historiadores actuales insisten en que condenado por la Inquisición equivale a judaizante, los contemporáneos de las víctimas no aceptaron tan unánimemente esa ecuación, alegando que era el odio contra los conversos y la codicia de sus bienes lo que movía al tribunal, no el celo por la fe.

Cosas que, aunque las gentes las saben, las pudren en su corazón, por temor

8. Los procedimientos de la inquisición castellano-aragonesa fueron objeto de numerosas críticas contemporáneas, procedentes del mismo papa, de la corte real y de particulares. Si no cuestionaron en cuanto tal la inquisición de herejes, destacaron los inconvenientes derivados de su carácter sumario y el que se dependiera de testigos fantasma, y del arbitrio de un inquisidor protegido por el secreto. Es cierto que sus juicios se ajustaban a derecho común en tanto que su carácter sumario era justificado por la gravedad del delito de herejía. Pero cuando esa modalidad excepcional se volvió procedimiento masivo, rutinario y permanente, numerosos inconformes protestaron, en lo posible, alegando que tan inusitada rigidez era contraria al derecho común y natural, y que, con gran frecuencia, violentaba usos y costumbres admitidos por consenso inmemorial o por fueros reales. La repulsa, como han destacado los estudiosos a partir de Lea, fue especialmente aguda en Aragón.

Una de las más notables víctimas tempranas, el arzobispo Talavera, de Granada, confesor de Isabel la Católica, fue denunciado por una

---

41. García Cárcel, *Orígenes...*, p. 170.

profetisa aprehendida por el inquisidor Lucero, antiguo enemigo del arzobispo. Según la vidente, el prelado, sus hermanas y los altos oficiales de su curia episcopal conspiraban para imponer el judaísmo en toda España. Talavera murió al día siguiente de desfilar descalzo, al lado de los suyos, en un auto de fe en Córdoba, en 1507. Meses antes, se había quejado ante el rey de las afrentas de los inquisidores, exigiendo que

"se procediese en todo conforme a derecho"; y a los acusados, "darles los nombres de los testigos [...] e darles lugar a que puedan apelar por justas causas [...] e todas las otras cosas que los derechos mandaron que se diesen al reo para se defender". Porque los inquisidores "siguen sus procesos por su tela de juicio, y a otros han fatigado y fecho muchas extorsiones para les hacer decir e confesar por diversas maneras non permisas en derecho [...], de donde resulta mucha sospecha contra los que lo facen, y mucho daño a los presos, y mucha infamia a los deudos [...]"[42].

Protestas análogas llegaron a los monarcas y a la curia romana. De una u otra forma, ambos admitieron que se trataba de un rigor desusado. Ya en 1481, apenas instaurado el tribunal en Sevilla, Sixto IV manifestó al rey que los jueces, *nullo juris ordine servato procedentes, multos injuste carceraverint, no (sic!) bonis spoliaverint, qui ultimo supplicio affecti fuere*[43], e intentó, sin excesivo celo, que se adoptaran los procedimientos ordinarios. El monarca replicó que, acceder a tales indultos, era dejar a los conversos *in eorum erroribus persistere*. En otras palabras, que la eficacia del tribunal derivaba de su excepcionalidad.

A la muerte de Fernando, en las cortes de Valladolid de 1518, Carlos V aceptó una reforma de fondo, obra del canciller Le Sauvage. Su inesperada muerte permitió al otro bando bloquear la firma real de esas

---

42. Llorente, *Historia crítica...*, Apéndice IX, vol. IV, pp. 294-297; Lea, I, pp. 220 y ss.

43. Llorente, *ibid*, Apénd. I, p. 267. Al año siguiente, el papa intentó prohibir *quatenus iuris communi contraria et ab eo aliena existant*: Apénd. II, p. 269. Y en otro breve del mismo 1482, se hacía eco de las quejas de que a los inquisidores los movía *non zelo fidei et salutis animarum sed lucri cupiditate*: Lea, I, pp. 845-49, y les ordenaba proceder conjuntamente con el ordinario, dando los nombres de sus acusadores a los detenidos y a sus abogados, admitir las legítimas excepciones respecto de los testigos, etc. La respuesta del rey, auténtica afirmación de una razón de estado, también en Lea, pp. 850-51.

medidas, cuyo encabezado es una abierta admisión, por parte del poder, de las graves consecuencias de tales procedimientos:

> la forma y orden que se ha tenido y tiene en el proceder de la dicha S*anta Inquisició*n, y de las causas tocantes a ella, ha sido y es tan estrecha y áspera, y con tanto secreto y encerram*ie*nto, que se ha dado ocasión y causa a que ayan avido muchos falsos testimonios *y dado lugar a la malicia y dolo de algunos malos officiales y ministros*, por los quales, y por los acusados no haver podido ser plenamente deffendidos… han padecido muchos innocentes y no culpados, daños y hapressiones, injurias y afrentas intolerables, fatigas, y sus hijos y hijas y descendientes, orfandad y ocasión de caer y exceder en otros muchos crímines y excesos, y muchos nuestros vassayos se han ido y ausentado destos reynos…[44]

De las 39 medidas tomadas entonces "para remediarlo", 32 tenían que ver con los juicios, y el resto con los bienes de los reos. En adelante, los jueces habrían de ser "hombres nobles y no pobres", de ciencia y conciencia, y ya no se les pagaría de "condenaciones"; cada dos años serían visitados por jueces ajenos al tribunal, y quienes cometiesen excesos, recibirían castigo y no sólo cambio de plaza. En cuanto a los testigos, sus nombres se publicarían, así como las acusaciones; y si eran enemigos, no valdría su testimonio. Tocante a los presos, pasarían a "cassas públicas" que fuesen "para guarda y no para pena", con derecho a recibir sacramentos, y a ser visitados por parientes, deudos y letrados, y éstos serían elegidos a voluntad. El tormento sería moderado, "conforme a los indiçios y provanças", sin recurrir "a ásperas y nuevas invenciones de tormentos", como venían usándose; sin reiterarlo, de no haber nuevas pruebas, y a nadie se aplicaría "para que diga de otro". En cuanto a los bienes, que sólo fuesen inventariados, sin confiscarlos, venderlos ni darlos a terceros por merced antes de que se

---

44. A H N-M, Inq. lib. 254, h. 68-72. Se trata de una copia de mediados del XVI, pues el amanuense, autor de los subrayados, cita al margen del cap. 18 – sobre que se publiquen los nombres de los testigos –, una bula de Paulo III, de 1549, acotando que el escrito papal se manifestaba "en esa misma conformidad". Por tratarse de un documento interno del tribunal, una apostilla así, es evidencia de que el debate seguía vivo en el seno del mismo. Al inicio del pasaje que cito, donde el amanuense escribió "la *fama* y orden", corregí por "forma". El documento, extractado por Lea (v. I., pp. 238-239) y citado a partir de él por muchos, parece seguir inédito.

tratara de "cosa juzgada". Que en el ínterin, pudiesen disponer de ellos para su sostenimiento, el de su familia, y para letrados, y que al condenado con hijos no se le privaría del derecho a heredarlos, consagrado en las Partidas. En suma, que en adelante se guardarían los cánones "de derecho común y canónico", sin nuevos estilos.

Es cierto que una reforma como la ensayada por Le Sauvage en 1518 no tuvo aplicación, y que pudo ser fruto de sobornos[45]; pero fue solicitada no sólo por conversos, sino por las cortes de Valladolid. Sucesos como los ocurridos en Córdoba poco antes, probaron que un inquisidor sin escrúpulos como Lucero, contando con apoyo real, no se limitaría a juzgar conversos, así fuesen arzobispos: ni los más encumbrados cristianos viejos, mientras tuviesen bienes, se librarían del cargo de judaizar, del despojo y de la hoguera. En la exposición de motivos de ese decreto fallido, se habló de juntas tenidas con letrados y doctos, y que el tema se había discutido en "estudios y collegios estudios generales, ansí de nuestros señoríos como de fuera dellos", debate del que no se tiene otra noticia. A raíz de esa consulta, en la más alta esfera política se admitió de forma abierta que, debido al "orden" seguido por el tribunal, en varios procesos habían "padecido muchos inocentes y no culpados". En suma: así en la corte regia como en la papal se calificaba netamente de anómala la situación. Si a pesar de reconocimientos tan expresos, las autoridades civiles y eclesiásticas no reformaron un estado de cosas por todos sabido, fue porque pesaron más el partido anticonverso y la razón de estado.

9. De modo análogo, numerosos particulares tuvieron clara noción de esa maquinaria, aunque callasen, por interés o por miedo. Entre los testimonios adversos al santo tribunal, destaca el de un clérigo de Toledo, escrito en 1538[46], por la sistemática y virulenta crítica de todo

---

45. Así afirmó Pedro Mártir, cit. por Lea, v. I, p. 239.

46. El memorial, antes citado repetidas veces (AHN, Inq. lib. 1325), fue objeto de agudo estudio por el malogrado M. Avilés Fernández, "Motivos de crítica a la Inquisición en tiempos de Carlos V (aproximaciones para una historia de la oposición a la Inquisición)", en Pérez Villanueva, (Ed.), *La Inquisición española...*, pp. 165-192. Aunque anunciaba su inminente publicación, parece no haberla realizado. Los indudables ecos erasmistas del lenguaje del autor del memorial, su evidente familiaridad con la corte imperial así como la aparente circunstancia de que hubiese viajado por otras naciones, me mueven a sugerir que se trata de Juan de Vergara. Quien haya sido el autor, parece haber vivido desde dentro la suerte que corrían los presos en las cárceles inquisitoriales, y Vergara, en esas mismas fechas, estaba sufriendo en carne propia las secuelas de un proceso y encarcelamiento. Pero antes de ir más lejos, se impondría encontrar evidencias firmes.

su procedimiento y de las consecuencias que acarreaba. El anónimo autor es evidentemente culto, muy ligado a la corte imperial, con la que quizás viajó fuera de España, y afín, o miembro, de los círculos erasmistas, pues en varios lugares, el eco del roterodamo se hace evidente, como cuando se insiste en por qué tanto odio y ánimo de venganza, si "nuestra santa fe es ley de graçia y no de rrigor" (h.18, h.15). Al parecer, conocía los Comentarios de Vives a la Ciudad de Dios, o al menos los pasajes de Agustín contra la tortura[47]. A momentos, parece seguir el *De concordia et discordia* del valenciano. De no ser el caso, se explicaría por el hecho de que ambos hablaban análogo lenguaje. Después de su lectura, es imposible seguir afirmando que los coetáneos carecían de elementos para ofrecer una interpretación coherente de la actuación del tribunal, alejada de la oficial.

Para el memorialista anónimo – cuyo escrito extracto aquí y allá –, si el rey "no lo rreforma, no faltarán en el Sancto Officio culpados; cómo o de qué manera, justa o injustamente: dios es el savidor" (h. 16-16vº). En efecto, si los inquisidores fuesen santos, no habría qué temer, pero "son hombres [...] y aun muchos dellos, labradores, nasçión muy contraria de los conversos: que ha avido ynquisidor dellos que decía: 'dámelo converso y darle e quemado', y otros que han tenido por opinión que ningún confesso puede ser buen christiano" (h. 15).

Tampoco faltarían culpables mientras el sustento de los inquisidores dependiera de las multas impuestas, y no de bienes de la iglesia o de la real hacienda: "rreçia cossa es que, si no queman, no comen [...] y ¿quién muere de hambre?", porque, como se ha visto, "para cobrar su salario, jamás les faltó culpados"(h. 16vº). Ni dejaría de haberlos "per secula fin", mientras una vida como buen cristiano valiera menos que el confuso "yndicio" aportado por "la triste mujercilla y el pobre rústico" o por testigos "para dañar", sea por venganza, o porque se los compró "a tres blancas" para decir cualquier atrocidad (h. 15 y 16). Tanto así, "que el arçobispo de Granada [el arriba mencionado, Talavera], que fue sancto, tubo dizque cinquenta testigos contra sí que depusieron que fue erege, y fue bentura no quemalle" (h. 16vº).

Siendo que "en este Sancto Oficio, a donde tanto ba, que es fama y bida y onra y hacienda de todo un linaxe y, aún a las bueltas, las almas", por qué ocultarles los testigos y privarlos de defensas, cuando "antes se les avían de añidir [...] que no quitársclas"(h. 18vº).

---

47. Ver, adelante, el § 13.

Porque – argüía –, siendo tan grave el crimen de herejía, "por negras, buenas provanças y claríssimas, se deven quemar los honbres, que no por presunciones vanas"(h. 19v°). En cambio, son detenidos "por lixeros indicios y por cosas muy livianas", o por expresiones *impromptu*, que no es dado controlar, y se remediarían con confesión o contrición simple. O también se toman "por cerimonias, [cosas] que ni lo fueron ni lo son" (h. 14v°). Una vez en el calabozo, sin vista de parientes ni de amigos, y sin sacramentos, pasan de uno a cuatro años, en lo que se reúne el número suficiente para montar un auto de fe. Ahí, creyéndose perdidos, "desesperados que no les vale la verdad", y atemorizados día a día para que confiesen, tanto los fuertes como los débiles "se rinden y destruyen a sí y a todos quantos se les antoxa, por vivir" (h. 14v°).

A continuación, se montan unos "autos ponposos [...] con mucho estruendo de ganapanes", como si se fuera "a canonicar un santo", pero que solo sirven "para desonrrar a España y destruir gentes" (h. 17v°). Así, se pregona "en toda la christiandad, que hubo un auto en Toledo de zient ereges, y pudo ser que no obo dos ni uno que se pudo deçir verdaderamente erege" (h. 15). El cuestionamiento de los métodos y de los resultados no podía ser más explícito, ni más amargo el escepticismo respecto de que en verdad fuesen culpables los así condenados.

En cambio, aquello sólo acarreaba la "mengua de Hespaña" porque "todas las naciones estranxeras nos llaman marranos" (h. 15). Peor aún – decía al monarca –:

Mira señor q*ue* en otras naçiones ay honbres riquíssimos que bastan para socorrer a v*uestra* m*agesta*d en tiempo de neçesidad, y con v*uestra* m*agesta*d se enrriqueçen; pues honbres más ábiles ay en España, sino que ninguno llega al gallinero, que los cortan en agraz, que muy pocos se escapan tarde o temprano de la sancta Ynquisiçión; porque [...], ¿quién hay tan bienquisto que, en comedio de toda su vida, le falte un enbidioso que le heche al hondo? Y mira, señor, que el más baleroso, el más justiçiero [...], el que más hávil es en ganar haçienda, esos tienen el mayor peligro, y essos son los que no se escapa ninguno deste laço; *en especial los conversos, que no escapa ninguno*. Ya s*eño*r no es tan gran cosilla que de Santa Ynquisi*ci*ón se a buelto en bengança de enemigos, sepoltura de honbres rricos, conorte [=consuelo] para enbidiosos (h. 16, r°/v°).

Y no sólo se estaba arruinando España en lo material:

> los predicadores no ossan predicar, y ya que predican, no se ossan meter en cossas sotiles, porque en la boca de dos nesçios está su bida y honra [...]. Que ay doctores ynabilitados en n*uest*ra España que bastarían para confundir a Lutero. Y se an ydo a rreynos estraños a mostrar su grandeça de letras, y en España no osan hablar, y los padres no osan que aprendan los hijos sancta theología por este temor. Y sin falta bendrá España en mucha diminución de letras en esta çiençia (h. 16).

Precisamente cuando las autoridades leían el memorial, estaban cumpliendo penitencia, luego de sus repectivos procesos, los teólogos apologistas de Erasmo, Juan de Vergara y el benedictino Alonso Virués[48]. No sólo los conversos estaban siendo víctimas del tribunal: todo aquél que mostraba alguna "grandeça de letras", o se le inhabilitaba, en caso de ser teólogo, o se callaba o huía del reino. La alusión al exilio por motivos de orden intelectual, es manifiesta. Vives se referirá, en términos análogos y con idéntica amargura, al terror imperante en su patria, que imponía silencio a los doctos[49].

También en Vives se percibe un análogo repudio al espíritu vindicativo del tribunal, así como a sus métodos y consecuencias, si bien el valenciano se expresa con mayor cautela y a lo largo de afirmaciones un tanto dispersas. Por otra parte, mientras el clérigo toledano se contentaba con pedir apremiantemente al emperador la reforma del tribunal, en Vives se desarrolla una reflexión de orden general sobre las causas de la discordia y de la concordia humana, y propone alternativas para una sociedad armónica, en donde no quepan la inhumanidad de la tortura ni el exilio.

III. ¿PEREGRINACION O EXILIO?

10. Como planteé al inicio del presente trabajo, una vez probado el origen social judeoconverso de Vives y la trágica suerte de su familia ante la Inquisición, resulta evidente el nexo entre su exilio y esa circunstancia capital, si bien, como indiqué, apenas si se ha reflexionado acerca del sentido que aquel drama tuvo para él. Por lo mismo, antes de

---

48. Para las vicisitudes del erasmismo en España, es aún imprescindible, M. Bataillon, *Erasmo y España,* Trad. de Antonio Alatorre, México, FCE, 1966.
49. Ver, adelante, el § 14.

recoger sus esporádicas afirmaciones o insinuaciones sobre el asunto, creí indispensable el rodeo que acabo de realizar. Primero, revisando el marco historiográfico, con frecuencia estrecho, que suele reducir el problema judeoconverso a la cuestión de si judaizaban o no los procesados por la Inquisición. Señalé que, más allá de la estricta cuestión religiosa, casos como el de Vives hay que situarlos como muestra de la violenta pugna social que estalló, a comienzos de la época moderna, entre dos estamentos de la sociedad hispana, el compuesto por los cristianos tradicionales o "viejos", y el de los antiguos hebreos, obligados por la fuerza a dejar su religión y sus hábitos ancestrales. En segundo lugar, y con el fin de dar el debido realce a lo manifestado por Vives sobre la persecución a los suyos y su exilio, me referí a las circunstancias que en su tiempo rodeaban al proceso inquisitorial, en tanto que arma fundamental de los cristianos viejos contra los nuevos[50]. Asimismo, documenté el hecho de que numerosos contemporáneos – tanto particulares como personalidades de las más altos medios civiles y eclesiásticos – manifestaron, con toda claridad, que el tribunal, en su marco jurídico y en sus actos, no se limitaba a la desinteresada búsqueda de la verdad. Resta ahora exponer, al trasluz de las previas consideraciones, lo que Vives escribió acerca de su exilio.

De entrada, conviene señalar que jamás se dictó en contra de Vives una sentencia formal de extrañamiento, ni él salió huyendo, como otros conversos, incluidos parientes suyos, para evadir una orden de arresto y el consiguiente proceso. Los suyos, en tanto que bautizados a raíz de las matanzas de 1391, tampoco fueron alcanzados por los decretos de expulsión de 1492.

Todo indica más bien que su alejamiento inicial de la patria, en 1509, para estudiar en la universidad de París, fue un acto de peregrinación académica, fenómeno aún frecuente entre estudiantes europeos. Sus posteriores visitas y el asentamiento definitivo en los Países Bajos, habrían tenido el propósito de buscar fortuna en la corte del futuro Carlos V, tal vez como secretario de alguno de aquellos potentados, fuese español o flamenco. Hay indicios de que hubiera vuelto a la península

---

50. Puede replicarse que la Inquisición no se limitó a perseguir a coversos y que, muy pronto, extendió su campo a otras herejías. Pero todo en su inicial conformación remite a ellos, y ellos fueron las víctimas casi exclusivas hasta la tercera década del XVI. Tampoco invalida esta afirmación el dato de que varios conversos hayan pertenecidoa la plantilla del tribunal: por más que ellos actuaran – a veces con singular saña – del lado de los perseguidores, la nómina de los perseguidos no por esto varió.

de habérselo demandado un empleo atractivo[51]. Es muy probable que, ya entonces, hubiese sido mal vista su condición de *confesso*, pero no era excepcional el retorno de conversos a la patria en pos de mejor fortuna. Se hallaba ahí "procurando", antes que exiliado.

En cambio, a raíz del último proceso inquisitorial contra su padre, en 1522 y que, luego de dos años, concluyó en la hoguera, Vives empezó a referirse a *Hispania nostra* con creciente amargura y hostilidad, y describió una situación semejante a la suya con el inequívoco nombre de exilio. Así pues, hubo que esperar mucho tiempo después de su alejamiento físico de la patria para que se operara en él un cambio de actitud. Al optar por el autoextrañamiento, según veremos, esperaba escapar a una suerte como la del padre, pero también, asegurarse condiciones de vida que le garantizaran independencia intelectual, que él consideraba irrenunciable[52]. Sobre todo porque, precisamente en esos años, la Inquisición, aparte de los conversos, empezó a perseguir también a los sospechosos de luteranismo o de comulgar con las ideas de un escritor tan polémico como su maestro, Erasmo de Rotterdam.

Delación y silencio

11. Los padres de Vives, ambos de Valencia, se desposaron en 1492. No es tarea fácil seguir sus vicisitudes ante la Inquisición, por la forma fragmentaria como sus procesos han llegado hasta nosotros, y el carácter tan híbrido de su composición. Dado que a cada preso se le exigía la delación de conocidos y parientes, al abrirse causa contra otro de los denunciados, el fiscal extraía esos testimonios previos para emplearlos como cargos en el nuevo proceso.

---

51. Estoy concluyendo un trabajo sobre los primeros años de Vives en las Países Bajos, y sobre sus contactos en la corte de Bruselas. A partir de Bonilla, los biógrafos se han referido a algunas ocasiones en que Vives habría contemplado volver a la península: con el cardenal Croy, arzobispo de Toledo; como instructor de los hijos del duque de Alba; o como catedrático de gramática en Alcalá. Los tres casos, anteriores a la ejecución de su padre.

52. En una carta, sin fecha, a Juan de Vergara, Vives le explicó su retiro de Inglaterra, durante la crisis del divorcio de Enrique VIII y Catalina, como cuestión de principios: rey y reina le exigían un comportamiento que iba contra sus convicciones, pero éstas valían para él tanto o más que el mandato de cualquier monarca: *mihi mea ratio instar est omnium principum*. En, *Epistolarum farrago*, Amberes, 1556, h.37 r°.

Al parecer, el sumario contra el padre se perdió, pero quedan importantes fragmentos[53]. En cuanto al seguido contra la madre, fue montado a veinte años de su muerte, con el evidente fin de que la Inquisición recuperase los 10,000 sueldos de dote, reclamados por las hijas tras el decomiso y pérdida de los bienes paternos. Por eso, es un agregado póstumo de piezas diversas, extraídas de su abjuración durante los edictos de gracia y de trozos de procesos a terceros, más los interrogatorios a tres presas que, hallándose en curso el proceso contra Blanca, coincidieron en recordar delitos cometidos por ella hacía "xxxxii o xxxxiii anys poch mes o menys"[54].

Todo intento de reconstruir la biografía espiritual de sus padres, debe hacer frente a esos fragmentos, amasados para "probar" que eran culpables de herejía. Si, con toda reserva, puede sacarse algo de ellos, habría que centrarse en la única pieza realmente testimonial, aunque engendrada por el miedo: la autoinculpación de la aún doncella Blanca March, en 1491, para acogerse al edicto de gracia, y un testimonio previo de inocencia, de 1487. Si en éste, dictado a los 14 años, se había declarado ajena a toda práctica indebida, en la confesión de 1491, dijo que a la "edat de nou anys poch mes o menys" (1480-81), su madre mandó a ella y a su hermana hacer el ayuno del perdón, que practicaron por dos años. Después se les advirtió – prosigue – "que no ffesem mes

---

53. El problema se complica por el afán de ocultamiento de algunos estudiosos. El señor Palacio, en su prólogo a los *Procesos* contra la madre del humanista, cita algunos documentos y promete otros, que jamás editó, omitiendo sus fuentes de archivo; A. García, en *Els Vives...*, aunque menciona unas cuantas signaturas en sus notas, ninguna de las que verifiqué en el AHN-M correspondía a los documentos por ella referidos.

54. De la Pinta, *Procesos...*, p. 49, y *passim*. Se trata de piezas de 1487, 1491, 1500, 1518, y 1527 a 1529; una de las actas había servido para procesar a una Sibila Ferrer; el escribano se limitó a tachar el nombre original, sustituyéndolo por el de la madre de Vives, pp. 66-68. La insistencia en los 43 años no era incidental: en 1487, Blanquina, acogida al edicto de gracia, declaró no haber incurrido en faltas contra la fe; en cambio, en 1491 – en vísperas de su boda – acudió al tribunal a abjurar de haber realizado el ayuno del perdón a los 9 años: tal vez para que, debidamente absuelta, pudiese recibir la dote sin riesgo de ulterior confiscación. La estrategia del Santo Oficio fue – 43 años después de la confesión de inocencia, y 39 después de la la abjuración – presentar testigos que aseguraran que "42 ó 43 años" atrás – es decir, con anterioridad a su absolución de 1491 –, ella había cometido delitos no confesados entonces ni después, con lo que su absolución resultaba dolosa y nula. Su dote, en consecuencia, la había adquirido en calidad de hereje, y debía ser retenida por el tribunal. Por eso la sentencia, de 1530, la condenó a perder los bienes adquiridos *tempus quadraginta trium annorum et inde* (pp 86).

lo dit dejuni por quant era venguda ja la Inquisitió en Valencia [...] e del temps que vench lo Reverent micer Galbes per Inquisidor [...] tinch intenció de viure e de morir com a tan solita christiana". Al preguntársele si sabía que el ayuno y demás prácticas eran cosas judaicas, "dix que no, per quant pensava que tot lo mon ho fechia axi". Recordó también que su madre leía un libro en hebreo, y un día, con su hermana, lo tomaron en sus manos, pero "non entenyem res, com fos en ebraych". Por otra parte, ya en 1487 había podido declarar el credo[55]. Lo poco que se sabe del padre, deja suponer circunstancias análogas, si bien él, como varón, se movía en círculos más amplios que el doméstico. En 1500, se le acusó de haber blasfemado de la Virgen en 1469, de 16 años... Otros cargos son tan tópicos como los atribuidos a la esposa[56].

El panorama esbozado recuerda el propuesto por Netanyahu en sus conclusiones, obtenidas a partir de otro género de fuentes[57]. Suponiendo que los conversos hubieran judaizado con cierta facilidad en Valencia antes de la Inquisición, la tradición religiosa iba diluyéndose de una generación a otra: si la abuela de Vives aún leía en hebreo, la madre y tía ya ignoraban la lengua sagrada. Prácticas religiosas reducidas al mínimo: Blanca no se autoinculpa de guardar el sábado, pero sí de un ayuno anual, a partir de cierta edad y cuando el riesgo era moderado. La llegada de la Inquisición – prueba de su eficacia disuasoria –, inhibe más las viejas prácticas y, con el pragmatismo impuesto por el terror, se opta en exclusiva, al menos formalmente, por el cristianismo, cuyos rezos sabían los hijos. Y si por caso, en especial aquellos

---

55. *Ibid.*, pp. 40-44.

56. AHN-M, Inq., leg. 5311, n° 21; se trata de dos hojas sueltas, recopiladas en 1523; en el mismo legajo, n° 57, hay 12 hojas más, con los testigos de cargo, que depusieron en su contra entre 1500 y 1520; el primer interrogatorio, de 6.10.1522; y la acusación, en 13 capítulos, contenía un solo cargo específico: sepultar a la mujer en tierra virgen; los demás, eran harto genéricos: blasfemó contra la Virgen en 1500, practicaba el ayuno del perdón, los sábados, diversos "ritos" y, cargo n° xiii: "otros muchos crímines y delictos hereticales". Él negó todo, en 24.11.1522, y se mantuvo en la negativa. Luego de una vasta laguna documental, las dos últimas hojas conservadas revelan que sólo al sufrir la prueba del tormento, en febrero de 1524, no resistió el dolor y se acusó. En el AARV, Mestre Racional, hay otros datos sobre bienes confiscados, lo que se pagó por el auto de fe, por alimentos de los presos y por el abogado, y lo que redituó la venta de las ropas despojadas a los ajusticiados en el patíbulo, el 6.9.1524; ver en especial los volúmenes n° 8325 y 8350.

57. Ver, arriba, el § 3.

conversos crecidos antes de la introducción del Santo Oficio, iniciaban a los más jóvenes en ciertas ceremonias, éstos carecían de plena conciencia de transgresión.

La falta de discernimiento de los niños entre prácticas lícitas y punibles, debió coartar aún más, por riesgosa, su iniciación en ritos judaicos. Ante la acusación de que, por 1500, Blanca había dicho a terceros creer que el mesías no era llegado, el defensor replicó lo inverosímil del cargo, hallándose entonces preso su marido, y cuando "lo dit Sanct Ofici stava en tanta fervor, que qualsevol convers stava tan atemorysat que no gosava parlar de les coses que fossen contra la fe". Si padres e hijos se estaban acusando entre sí – argüía –, ¿cómo creer que alguien confiaba cosas tan graves a terceros que no eran ni parientes inmediatos?[58]

De admitir esas premisas, cabría plantear que Vives – nacido durante los años más álgidos de la Inquisición, y con su familia bajo permanente acoso, entre la cárcel y la hoguera – difícilmente fue iniciado en los secretos de la fe proscrita, hubiese sido por cautela o por sinceridad de los padres. El defensor de Blanca y los testigos de descargo coincidieron en describirla como "dona molt gentil, la qual exía molt poch de casa per sa honestat, *e per complaure al diyt son maryt*, molt poch conversava ab algú, sino en anar los dies dels dumenges e festes a myssa"[59]. Las declaraciones del defensor coinciden con lo manifestado por Vives acerca de los suyos: gran armonía conyugal, fundada en la constante disposición de la esposa a complacer al marido[60]. En ese trasfondo de silencio y pavor, cobra pleno sentido la anécdota de Vives,

---

58. Pinta, *Procesos...*, pp. 73-74.

59. Pinta, *Procesos...*, pp. 73-78, subrayado mío.

60. En este campo, como en otros, la falta de una edición crítica del *De institutione Christianae foeminae* dificulta las precisiones. Vives dijo a Erasmo haber comenzado el tratado en agosto de 1522, y lo dedicó a la reina en abril del año siguiente; es decir, durante su redacción dio comienzo el proceso final contra el padre, aprehendido en octubre de 1522. En el libro II, en un pasaje sobre armonía conyugal, menciónó a ambos progenitores por sus nombres, con anécdotas y vivos elogios, párrafo que el propio Vives eliminó en la edición definitiva, de Basilea, 1538 (*Príneps*, n° 22), por lo que tampoco aparece en los *Opera*, de 1555; en cambio, Mayans lo habría incluido, al adoptar la edición príncipe de Hillen, 1524 (*Príneps*, n° 21). Si ya en la edición madrileña de 1792, de la versión castellana del libro, se llamaba la atención sobre la importancia de esas variantes, todavía hoy traducciones como la del Ayuntamiento de Valencia, 1994, no obstante su vistosa apariencia, siguen al margen de toda preocupación crítica.

según la cual, su madre, hasta tal punto no sonreía ni era blanda, que se creyó no amado por ella, al grado de huir de casa por unos días. Blanca enfermó de pena con la ausencia, pero fue tan poco expresiva al retorno del hijo, que él imaginó que no había sufrido por su ausencia, y la odió con pasión[61]. Ante el ubicuo riesgo de la delación, sólo el silencio sobre lo que ocurría en los afectos y en las conciencias era sano.

Surge el exilio

12. La noticia de la prisión del padre alcanzó a Vives en un momento particularmente crítico, en diciembre de 1522. El año precedente había muerto el joven cardenal Croy, arzobispo de Toledo y discípulo del humanista en Lovaina, a cuya sombra creía tener resueltos todos sus problemas financieros[62]. Vives había combatido, al lado de su maestro Erasmo, a los enemigos del humanismo, pero cuando el roterodamo se marchó de Lovaina, el valenciano encontró insoportables la ciudad y la docencia. Además, la mala venta de sus Comentarios había agriado un tanto las relaciones entre maestro y discípulo. Buscaba colocación al servicio del rey de Inglaterra cuando, casi a una con las nuevas sobre su padre, le llegó invitación para suceder a Nebrija en la cátedra de la universidad de Alcalá.

La correspondencia de esos momentos con Erasmo y, más aún, con Cranevelt, revela la angustia sufrida por Vives. No se sabe si, en privado, llegó a confesarles el auténtico drama; nunca mediante escrito conocido. En enero de 1523, escribió a Cranevelt que su único hermano varón había fallecido, y que su padre era afligido por tan grave enfermedad, que había pocas esperanzas; además, se seguía en su contra un "grandísimo y odiosísimo pleito de bienes"[63], a resultas del cual quedaban sus tres hijas, doncellas y pobres. Se quejó de los hados (*de fatis*) y de su incierta situación, pues mientras deliberaba sobre ir o no a Valencia, no tenía calma para otros asuntos. En marzo, le escribió de

---

61. *De institutione...*, en *Opera*, Basilea, 1555, vol. 2, p. 738. En *Joan Lluís Vives...*, propuse una interpretación de estos documentos que ahora matizo, pp. 95-103.

62. En la recién descubierta serie de cartas a Craneveldt, pueden verse las dramáticas circunstancias en que el suceso alcanzó a Vives: J. IJsewijn, With G. Tournoy, D. Sacré, L. IJsewijn-Jacobs, M. Mund-Dopchie, "Litterae ad Craneveldium Balduinianae, A Preliminary Edition, 2, Letters 31-55", *Humanistica Lovaniensia*, XLII, 1993, pp. 1-51; ep. 38, pp. 20-24.

63. H. de Vocht, *Literae virorum...*, Ep. 32, del 4.1.1523, pp. 86-87.

nuevo, desesperado. Lo llamaban por cartas; no quería ir, ni podía quedarse. Lo frenaban los gastos y el peligro lo disuadía. Se imaginaba más desdichado que Odiseo, quien en tantas tormentas seguía teniendo a dónde ir, mientras él navegaba sin otra dirección que el hado[64]. Luego, a principios de mayo, informó tanto a Erasmo como a Cranevelt que por ningún motivo había podido evitar el viaje; pero, a causa de la guerra (entre Francisco I y Carlos V) debía ir primero a la neutral Inglaterra para, de ahí, buscar navío a España. Añadía a Cranevelt que todo era noche y tinieblas, no tanto en las cosas, como en su espíritu y determinaciones.

Vives debió llegar a Inglaterra la primera quincena de mayo. De viajar a Valencia, lo que se ignora, habría sido una cortísima estancia, pues ya el 3 de julio circulaban noticias en Brujas acerca de la excelente acogida dispensada al humanista en la corte de Enrique[65]. En mayo de 1524, estuvo en Brujas, donde casó con su prima Margarita Valldaura, signo de que en la isla encontraba vientos favorables. Vuelto a ella en octubre, ahí lo alcanzaría la noticia de la relajación del padre, la abuela paterna, una tía materna y otra parienta. Casi al mismo tiempo, moría el tío Miquel Dixer, administrador del conde de Oliva, que en vano había intentado salvar de la hoguera a su cuñado. Vives anunció en diciembre la muerte de ese tío, que veía más por la casa de los Vives que por la suya propia. Tanto la fortuna lo golpeaba, que acabaría insensible a ella[66]. En cambio, sólo en enero siguiente, y por única vez, hay una alusión a Cranevelt sobre el fin del padre: la fortuna, semejante a ella misma, lo seguía golpeándolo al batir a su padre y a los suyos[67]. El joven alegre y un tanto afectado que revelan sus primeros escritos dio paso a un hombre grave, pero sin amargura, salvo al hablar de la patria.

La desdicha de los suyos ante la Inquisición no concluyó con la ejecución paterna. Cuando las hermanas, despojadas del patrimonio familiar, reclamaron y obtuvieron la dote de la madre que, por ley, no

---

64. *Ibid.*, ep. 38, del 15.3.<1523>, pp. 114-115.

65. Eso escribió J. de Fevyn a Cranevelt, el 3.7.<1523>, *ibid.*, ep. 63, p. 158. El propio Fevyn le comentó al mismo amigo, el 26.8 (Ep. 71, p.177), que Vives gozaba de condición digna en Londres. Luego, en noviembre, el valenciano anunciaba a Craneveld haberse establecido en Oxford (Ep. 80, p. 197).

66. *Ibid.*, 2.12.1524, ep. 128, p. 352.

67. *Ibid.*, 25.1.1525, ep. 136 p. 368. Noreña fue el primer biógrafo en interpretar esos dramáticos pasajes epistolares a la luz del los procesos inquisitoriales. A mi ver, no es necesario pensar que Vives se refería sólo a la Inquisición al hablar de su triste *fortuna*: era una suma de desgracias la que lo hacía sentirse un Ulises sin rumbo.

pertenecía al cónyuge, el Santo Oficio decidió recuperarla por la vía de condenar la memoria de la esposa. El proceso se abrió en septiembre de 1528, para culminar en enero de 1530, con la condena a pérdida total de los bienes de Blanca en favor del fisco real, y a que sus huesos, sepultados 22 años antes en Alcira, fuesen traídos a Valencia, para quemarlos ante la catedral.

La imagen que el humanista reivindicó de sus padres, mezcla de armonía conyugal y de rigor moral, aunque tal vez corroborada por las propias fuentes inquisitoriales, fue también un gesto de distanciamiento del hijo frente a las sentencias de herejía. Al dar comienzo el último de los juicios contra su padre, vimos que lo tachó de "pleito de bienes"; y cuando la memoria de la madre fue condenada, en 1530, no acató el veredicto, pues en la edición revisada de sus *Commentaria,* salida un año después, siguió sosteniendo: *Blancha mater matronarum omnium, nisi pietas fallit, pudicissima*[68].

A partir de la ejecución paterna, que condenaba a hijos y nietos a la infamia y a la exclusión de cargos públicos seculares y eclesiásticos, quedaba cancelada para Vives toda posibilidad de carrera en la península[69]; si por caso pensó en andar a Castilla el día que pasase a residir a Toledo el malaventurado cardenal Croy, en lo sucesivo Vives debería buscarse la patria en Inglaterra o los Países Bajos. Pero su prometedor futuro en el primer reino se truncó al optar por la causa de Catalina en el divorcio real[70], resultando insostenible su estancia en la isla a partir de 1528. Se recluyó, pues, en Brujas, que se había vuelto su Ítaca, y

---

68. Anotación aparecida en *De civitate dei...*, l. XII, c. 20. Cito las anotaciones de Vives a partir de la edición expurgada por los teólogos de Lovaina, Amberes, Plantin, 1576, vol. V (*Princeps,* nº 18), confrontada con la de París, Chevallon, 1531 (*Princeps,* nº 17) y con Basilea, 1522 (*Princeps,* nº16), a fin de detectar los pasajes revisados por el propio autor y los suprimidos después por la censura. En las tres, se lee el pasaje. Desato las abreviaturas y escribo *u* o *v* según el el sonido sea de vocal o consonante. Por su falta de suficiente aparato crítico y su desvinculación del texto agustiniano editado por Vives, la nueva edición valenciana de los Comentarios, en curso en *Opera omnia...*, vol. II y siguientes, no puede ser considerada, en sentido estricto, crítica.

69. Al no conservarse el fin del proceso contra el padre de Vives, no aparece la condena a la infamia contra los descendientes, que complementaba la sentencia. Véase, con todo, la dictada contra Jeroni, tío paterno del humanista, en J. Ventura, *Inquisició espanyola i cultura renaixentista al País Valenciá*, Valencia, Tres i Quatre, 1977, p. 191.

70. El mejor estudio sobre su periplo inglés, sigue siendo, H. de Vocht, "Vives and his Visits to England", en *Monumenta Humanistica Lovaniensia,* Lovaina, 1934, pp. 1-60.

donde, si no contaba con medios para una holgada manutención, vivían su esposa, sus parientes políticos, y tenía amigos, en especial varios canónigos de la colegial de san Donaciano. En adelante – si se exceptúan dos años pasados en Breda, al lado de la marquesa del Zenete – sobrevivió de la pluma y, tal vez, subsidiariamente del comercio.

El verdadero exilio y la auténtica patria

13. Durante el viaje de Carlos V a Italia en 1529, camino de su coronación imperial, aún volvió Vives a buscar fortuna, como en su juventud, en esa corte, pero sus valedores de entonces habían salido casi todos de escena, y no parece que obtuviera más de una módica pensión[71]. A su condición de *marrano* e hijo de condenado, se sumaba su fama de erasmista, en un momento en que los enemigos del roterodamo afianzaban posiciones. Con miras a ganar el favor del emperador, le dedicó, en julio de 1529, *De concordia et discordia*, un tratado en el que reflexionó sobre las condiciones generales que hacían posible o inviable la coexistencia de los hombres en tanto que animales políticos.

Luego de manifestar al monarca que se esperaba de él la obtención de la concordia entre los príncipes y, mediante un concilio, la concordia entre los cristianos, Vives expuso su idea central[72]. Para él – a tono

---

71. Carlos se embarcó en Barcelona en julio de 1529, suscitando grandes expectativas, de las que Vives se haría eco; sólo después de Italia, pasó a los Países Bajos, de enero de 1531 al enero siguiente (Foronda y Aguilera, *Estancias y Viajes de Carlos V*, Madrid, Fortanet, 1895, pp. 28-29). Precisamente en 1532, Vives anunció a Vergara la obtención de una pensión de 150 ducados que, de pagársele regularmente – cosa que ignoramos –, cubriría la mitad de sus gastos. A. Bonilla, "Clarorum Hispaniensium epistolae ineditae", en *Revue Hispanique,* VIII (1901), pp. 181-308; Vives a Vergara, 8.8.1532, p. 267.

72. La primera edición, *Príncipes*, n° 32. La idea central se repite en los cuatro libros, un tanto reiterativos, que componen el tratado o, quizás más bien, las cuatro declamaciones del género suasorio. Sin duda, el autor intenta mover al lector por todas las vías. Con todo y su carácter difuso, alcanzó dos traducciones alemanas en el XVI, y ha gustado a los traductores castellanos de este siglo, que lo han vertido en tres ocasiones: primero, por el republicano exiliado, L. Sánchez Gallego, México, Séneca, 1940; luego, por L. Riber, en las *Obras completas...,* II, 75-253; finalmente, E. Rivera de Ventosa, para Ediciones Paulinas, Madrid, 1978. Vives, en su polémica conra los judíos, escrita a modo de diálogo en *De veritate fidei christianae* (*Príncipes*, n° 46), nunca tocó el tema de los conversos. J. Gómez, en "El diálogo Contra iudaeos de Vives y su tradición medieval" (*Criticón,* 41 (1988), pp. 67-85), concluye que el valenciano prolonga una tradición medieval, sin alterar "la pauta seguida por los diálogos *contra iudaeos* medievales y, sobre todo, por los *Dialogi* de Pedro Alfonso. La diferencia más importante estriba en que Vives es más elegante literariamente". Mientras Alfonso abusa de los silogismos, Vives "intenta acercarse al conocimiento revelado con argumentos probables y no con argumentos necesarios", p. 77. Como buen humanista, se valía de la lógica probabilística, desarrollada por Valla y Agrícola y, por él mismo, no para imponer verdades a rajatabla, sino para persuadir.

con el humanismo de vena pacifista –, el fundamento de la vida social, es decir, de la convivencia humana, era la concordia. La discordia, en cambio, sólo acarreaba descomposición y ruina para pueblos, familias e individuos. La concordia – alegaba – congregó al género humano, fundó las ciudades y las dejó conservarse y crecer; descubrió las artes útiles para la vida, la obtención de riquezas y el cultivo de los ingenios, favoreciendo en grado sumo que éstos encontrasen buenas condiciones para el cultivo de la sabiduría, la erudición y la virtud. La discordia, al revés, dispersaba a los hombres, llevándolos a errar entre el miedo y la inseguridad. Destruía las ciudades, sus instituciones y las rutas para el comercio entre los hombres; desquiciaba lo bien asentado, trayendo guerras, disensiones civiles, hambre, epidemias, miseria, incompetencia, y echaba por tierra el cultivo de los saberes y de la virtud.

A su juicio, el origen de toda discordia se hallaba en el estallido incontrolado de las pasiones, lo que llegaba a afectar tanto a particulares como a príncipes o a pueblos. En consecuencia, así como todos participaban en la destrucción cuando eran presa de las pasiones, así también todos podían contribuir a la paz, aprendiendo a gobernar las suyas, y cumpliendo cada quien sus reponsabilidades con ánimo pacificador. Si la sociedad, en cada uno de sus estamentos, aprendía a vivir en concordia, todas las artes útiles para la vida y todas las diciplinas intelectuales florecerían. De ahí la importancia de la educación que, en última instancia, era tanto como enseñar el ejercicio de la concordia.

Lo expuesto en *De concordia et discordia* resulta consistente con dos opiniones expresadas antes por Vives en sus comentarios a san Agustín, en las que argumenta su rechazo a la actitud persecutoria contra los herejes y al empleo de la tortura judicial como medio para obtener confesiones de un detenido. Sin guardar relación inmediata con el tema de la Inquisición, conllevan una inequívoca condena a los usos del tribunal, pero asimismo a la ola de intolerancia desencadenada en Europa a raíz de la difusión de las polémicas ideas de Erasmo y, más aún, de la irrupción de Lutero.

Frente a la mentalidad beligerante y punitiva contra los herejes, razón de ser de instituciones como el Santo Oficio, Vives reivindicó la visión agustiniana del problema. El pasaje de la Ciudad de Dios donde dice Agustín que los cristianos pravos han de ser *correpti ut sanum rectumque sapiant* (XVIII, 51), fue glosado por su comentarista – en la mejor línea del humanismo – realzando la primacía de la educación: los herejes debían ser amonestados y enseñados en la sana doctrina cristiana, hasta comprenderla rectamente. Y así como Agustín manifestó que, si no querían corregirse, al menos hacían a la iglesia el bien de probar la paciencia de los justos, el humanista dijo que, a los renuentes, los perderían tanto su contumacia como sus perversas opiniones[73]. No habló pues de persecución, sino de tolerancia y de enseñarles recta doctrina.

El alegato de Vives contra la tortura se apoya también en san Agustín, quien lamentó que los jueces, por ignorar la mente de los acusados, recurrieran a testigos inocentes, torturados para averiguar la verdad en una causa que no les concernía. Más deplorable parecía al santo el empleo de la tortura en una causa propia, cuando, para saber si un indiciado era culpable, se le atormentaba, con lo que el inocente sufría penas certísimas por una culpa incierta. La ignorancia del juez era, así, la ruina del inocente, no por saber que tenía culpa, sino por desconocer su integridad. Pero lo que encontraba más intolerable, y que ameritaría ríos de llanto, era que el juez, al torturar a un inocente para saber si lo era, acabara enviádolo a morir, justo cuando quería evitarle el suplicio si no había faltado. Y si alguien prefería la muerte a seguir soportando el dolor, confesando lo que no hizo, el juez lo enviaba a tortura y ejecución por ignorarlo libre de falta (XIX,6).

Vives se vale del pasaje para una declaración de inusual vehemencia contra la tortura como medio para inquirir la verdad, recurso que declara invención de tiranos. Ante todo, la considera inútil, pues, quien es capaz de soportar el tormento, no revela la verdad, ni tampoco quien es incapaz. Como ya Publilio Sirio escribió: el dolor hace mentir también a los inocentes. Además, no se ejerce sin perjuicio de la república, pues ¿cómo no ha de ser nocivo atormentar a alguien de cuyo crimen se duda? Torturamos a los hombres, dice, para no matar inocentes, y mejor fuera la muerte que tal suplicio. No sólo porque a veces se mata con la tortura, sino porque el sufrimiento, o el temor a él, lleva a la víctima a confesar crímenes ficticios. Con toda nuestra humanidad – exclama –, tenemos ánimos carniceros para soportar los gemidos y gritos de delincuentes inciertos, llevados al tormento por sospechas o por denuncias de enemigos. Por fin, sobre inútil y nociva, la declara contraria, no sólo a la mansedumbre y caridad cristiana, sino a toda humani-

---

73. Para las ediciones de los Comentarios de Vives, ver nota 687. En las tres, se lee: *Admonendi sunt haeretici, ut melius sapiant, et ab ecclesia ex doctrina sana docendi parum esse christiana quae affirment; quod si audire nolint ecclesiam, non minus ipsi contumacia sua sibi oberunt quam scelestis opinionibus.*

dad, e ignora por qué necedad los cristianos se empeñan en tomarla por una práctica religiosísima[74].

La condena, tan inapelable como emotiva, era poco afín con la mentalidad general de la época, pero coincidía con lo expuesto por los críticos del Santo Oficio: al no servir el tormento para descubrir la verdad, tenía, en cambio funestas consecuencias, como la de castigar con gran crudeza a quien no necesariamente era infractor, o la de ocasionarle su ruina cuando, cediendo al dolor, se declaraba culpable de un delito imaginario. Un presunto delito originado con frecuencia en sospechas o denuncias de enemigos. El pasaje, a pesar de seguir tan de cerca a Agustín, fue eliminado por la censura. En la edición de los teólogos de Lovaina no aparece en el texto impreso; en los demás casos, o fue tachado a mano en numerosos de los ejemplares conservados, o se lee al margen la advertencia: *caute legatur*. Sin duda, al tratarse de una práctica común a varios tribunales, Vives la repudió en general, evitando una mención expresa de la Inquisición. Con todo, difícilmente tenía otra cosa en mente al indignarse de que se considerara al tormento una práctica *religiosissima,* siendo contrario a la caridad cristiana y a toda humanidad.

La primera edición de las anotaciones a la Ciudad de Dios salió a luz en 1522, meses antes de la prisión de su padre. Vives reiteró el pasaje en su versión revisada de 1531, luego de que aquél, cediendo al tor-

---

74. Dice Vives, edición de 1531: *Vere Superbi Tarquinii, aut etiam Tyrani hoc immanioris inventum, tormentis inquiri veritatem, quam nec qui pati poterit, proferit, nec qui pati non poterit, nam, ut ait prudens Mimus: etiam innocentes cogit mentiri dolor. Miror christianos homines tam multa gentilia, et ea non modo charitati et mansuetudini christianae contraria, sed omni etiam humanitati, mordicus tanquam religiosissima retinere.* Más adelante: *nec utilis est, et sine damno rerum publicarum tolli potest. Quomodo vivunt tam multae gentes, et quidem barbarae, ut Graeci et Latina putant, quae ferum et immane arbitrantur torqueri hominem de cuius facinore dubitatur? Nos homines omni videlicet humanitati praediti, sic torquemus homines ne insontes moriantur, ut magis eorum nos misereat quam si morerentur, usque adeo graviora sunt saepe tormenta, quam mors [...] Et fateantur ficto crimen de supplicio certi, ne torqueantur. Profecto carnifices animos habemus, qui sustinere possumus gemitus et lacrymas tanto cum dolore expressas hominis, quem nescimus sitne noscens. Quid quod acerbam perquam iniquam legem sinimus in capita nostra dominari cum suspiciones tormentis armamus, et inimicis delationibus?* [...] Y, prueba de las cosas que se dejó en el tintero, concluye: *Mihi non vacat ac ne libet quidem de tormentis hic loqui copiosius, cum possem, nec declamari magis videar, quam commentaria scribere. Locus est apud Rhetores communis de tormentis, et contra tormenta. Fortissima sunt quaecunque contra tormenti dicunt; quae vero pro tormentis, futilia et imbecilla.*

mento, se confesara hereje, y acabara en las llamas, y cuando los restos de su madre habían corrido pareja suerte, a partir de testimonios inducidos mediante tortura a tres ancianas prisioneras.

14. A modo de apéndice al *De concordia et discordia*, y con portada aparte, Vives escribió el opúsculo *De pacificatione*, dedicándolo a uno de los pocos cortesanos que aún permanecían en el entorno de Carlos desde su juventud: Alonso Manrique, conocido por el valenciano quince años atrás, pero que, en 1529, ya había sido promovido a arzobispo de Sevilla y a inquisidor general. El prelado se hallaba en la cumbre de su prestigio e influencia; además, entre sus servidores había amigos de Vives desde los años estudiantiles en París: Luis Coronel y el médico Juan Martín Población, lo que garantizaba al valenciano buenos mediadores ante Manrique. Recordando la antigua *familiaritas*, y nombrando a los conocidos comunes, Vives se atrevió a decir en letras de molde lo que otros susurraban de boca en boca o decían en textos anónimos. Siéndonos conocidas las opiniones del humanista sobre la tortura y sobre el trato que debía darse a los herejes, su admonición al inquisidor general cobra plena relevancia. Los deberes del arzobispo para contribuir a la pacificación del pueblo cristiano – le manifestó – venían de su triple condición de consejero real, de su dignidad episcopal, y de su cargo inquisitorial. En cuanto al último ministerio, lo prevenía del riesgo de pecar gravemente si olvidaba las obligaciones inherentes a oficio tan peligroso como el suyo, ya que de él pendían salud, fortuna, fama y vida de tantos. Acto seguido, ponía el dedo en la llaga, tocando los dos aspectos más cuestionados de la actuación del tribunal: le causaba gran extrañeza que, en una institución a tal punto delicada, se diera tanta mano al juez, no exento de pasiones humanas, y al acusador, que con frecuencia era movido a calumniar por odio, esperanza de lucro o cualquier otra depravada codicia de su ánimo[75].

Vemos pues cómo Vives, quien no dio signos de haber admitido en su fuero interno los veredictos de herejía fallados por el tribunal contra sus padres, de diversos modos puso en tela de juicio la eficacia, utili-

---

75. J. L. Vives, *Opera*, Basilea, 1555, II, p. 862. Manrique tiene a su cargo, por fin, el *munus inquisitionis haereticorum, quod quum tantum sit, tamque periculosum, nisi sciat quis quod pertineat eo peccabit gravius quod de plurium salute, fortunis, fama et vita agitur. Mira dictu res, tantum esse permissum vel iudici, qui non caret humanis affectionibus, vel accusatori, quem nonnunquam ad calumniam, odium, vel spes, vel prava aliqua impellit animi cupiditas.*

dad, honorabilidad y cristianismo de sus procedimientos. No se declaró partidario de la persecución a los herejes, sino de darles instrucción; encontró ineficaz, nocivo para la sociedad e inhumano, el empleo de la tortura para recabar confesiones; y por fin, halló que se concedía demasiada libertad a la pasión de los jueces, y excesivo crédito a la frecuente malevolencia o ignorancia de los testigos.

Esa acerba actitud crítica da pleno sentido a un extenso pasaje de Vives, incluido precisamente en *De pacificatione*, donde, hablando en tercera persona, parece ofrecernos la clave de su exilio como alejamiento voluntario de un clima social que imposibilitaba la sana convivencia entre ciudadanos, y el libre desarrollo del quehacer intelectual. Aseguró que, en una ciudad donde las pasiones de unos contra otros se hallaban exacerbadas, ningún ciudadano quedaba a salvo de la malevolencia de sus vecinos. Que semejante clima no era una patria, sino un exilio.

Entre los vecinos de una ciudad – argumentó –, no hay cosa más dulce que la concordia. Todo discurre en un ambiente amable. Tanto, que muchos hombres prudentes y experimentados, luego de ver tierras y mares, olvidando la patria, decidieron dar fin a su peregrinar ahí donde la quietud de las costumbres, de las leyes (*moribus atque instituto maiorum*), y la mansedumbre de los ingenios, permitiera vivir en paz. Tales hombres tienen su patria y sus parientes dondequiera que se cultiven la paz y la concordia, y se estimen las prendas y el nombre de todos.

Exilio, en cambio – proseguía –, es la ciudad donde el ciudadano se mete con los ciudadanos y habitantes. Donde el vecino, el curioso, el alborotador, molestan al vecino. Donde el prójimo, el amigo, el desconocido, buscan, por naderías, romper la quietud. No sólo es algo intolerable de sufrir sino de ver. Al grado de que muchos prefieren dejar casa, patria y mayores, y emigrar lejísimos "a donde nadie pueda tocar esas cosas (*earum rerum*), ni tenga de ellas conocimiento alguno, ni las haya visto, oído ni entendido". ¿Quién puede soportar con gozo unos odios entre conciudadanos y vecinos, sin advertir que "tarde o temprano, pero indudablemente, en algún momento se volverán en su contra"? ¿Quién puede enlistar el sinnúmero de daños que "aquellas interpretaciones siniestras" provocan en las ciudades? Odios, pleitos y un arte de malinterpretar las cosas según la áspera e inflexible regla de que "nada puede nadie hacer o decir, por recto, simple y circunspecto que sea, que no se le tome al instante en el peor de los sentidos"[76].

El pasaje deja pocas dudas. El propio Vives, como el hombre "prudente y experimentado" de su imagen, deja traslucir que su exilio tenía la finalidad principal de escapar a un medio hostil, a una persecución social que, con independencia de si concluía o no en un desenlace como el de su padre, imposibilitaba para él y los suyos toda forma de vida en paz.

Que el medio hostil aludido en ese texto, era la propia patria, lo revela sin ambages el valenciano en una carta privada, escrita en 1533, a raíz de que la Inquisición aprehendió a su amigo toledano, el humanista Juan de Vergara. Por desgracia, la propia carta de Vives no llegó hasta nosotros, sólo lo que respondió a ella su joven discípulo Rodrigo Manrique, uno de los hijos, por cierto, del inquisidor general. En un lugar, Manrique glosa lo que su preceptor le había escrito: "De plano, es cierto *lo que dices*, nuestra patria es soberbia y envidiosa; añade: y bárbara. Porque ahí ya se da por cierto que no hay un hombre medianamente formado en buenas letras al que no se puedan imputar herejías, errores, judaísmos. Tanto, que se ha impuesto el silencio a los doctos, y se ha inyectado, *como dices,* un ingente terror a cuantos tendían hacia la erudición"[77]. Su propia patria era pues esa "ciudad" donde predominaban la soberbia y la envidia, a más de la intolerancia intelectual. Y si en ella su origen social no encontraba aceptación, menos aún, la indispensable libertad para desarrollar la clase de pensamiento independiente y crítico por él reivindicado.

En consecuencia, a fin de encontrar un medio donde sus "prendas y buen nombre" tuvieran crédito, y donde su dedicación al estudio no lo convirtiera en sospechoso, Vives juzgó necesario mantenerse lejos de Aragón y Castilla, en cuyas coronas la Inquisición estaba al frente de la cruzada anticonversa y – a partir de la tercera década del siglo – también antierasmista y antiluterana. Aunque a la postre condenado a vivir en la pobreza, el humanista encontró en los Países Bajos, menos afecta-

---

76. Supongo que fue V. Sanz (*Vigencia actual de Luis Vives,* Montevideo, 1967, p. 33), el primero en advertir el trasfondo de este amargo pasaje. *Opera*, Basilea, 1555, II, p. 873. Riber, en las *Obras Completas*, v. II, pp. 274-75, lo tradujo en forma harto diluida y hasta incompleta.

77. H. de Vocht, "Rodrigo Manrique's Letter to Vives", en *Monumenta Humanistica Lovaniensia*, Lovaina, 1934, pp. 427- 458; el pasaje: *Plane uerum est quod dicis inuidam atque superbam illam nostram patriam; adde, & barbaram. Nam iam pro certo habetur apud illos neminem bonarum literarum mediocritur excultum, quin heresibus, erroribus, Judaismis sit refertus; ita ut doctis positum sit silentium; ijs uero qui ad eruditionem properabant iniectus, ut ais, ingens terror.* P. 435.

dos por aquel clima de acoso social e intelectual, y lejos de la jurisdicción del tribunal, condiciones favorables para desarrollar su obra escrita. No es, pues, gratuito que los hubiera llamado patria con reiteración.

De cualquier modo, su silencio en torno a la suerte de los suyos debía de ser total, así como la cautela para expresar sus ideas. Aunque tantas veces citada, viene al caso la frase escrita a Erasmo acerca de que vivían tiempos tan difíciles, que no era posible hablar ni callar sin peligro. En especial porque, siendo él un intelectual, y más aún, de las filas de Erasmo, cuyas ideas empezaron a ser objeto de polémica antes incluso de que surgiera Lutero, en 1517, toda falta de prudencia podría conducirlo a un proceso en el que fácilmente se mezclaran las acusaciones de heterodoxia con sus antecedentes familiares.

El expatriado y el pensador

15. En el exilio de Vives convergían, por tanto, razones de índole social e intelectual. Y dado que los Países Bajos le ofrecían las dos condiciones que él explícitamente consideraba irrenunciables para una vida aceptable: tolerancia social y libertad para el estudio, queda, por último, formular la pregunta de ¿en qué sentido se entrelazan en Vives el exiliado y el intelectual? De nuevo, la respuesta no es fácil. El humanista Vives no se exilió por sus ideas. Al abandonar, joven, la patria, en busca de letras y fortuna, difícilmente tenía ya un pensamiento definido, y menos aún, crítico. La circunstancia de haber pertenencido a un grupo minoritario, a la vez laico y urbano, y perseguido hasta el exterminio, iría matizando su pensamiento a medida que éste cobraba forma en contacto con las influencias que sus sucesivos domicilios le iban ofreciendo: primero, la "sutil" escolástica parisiense; luego, ahí mismo, el humanismo italianizante; por fin, en Lovaina, el humanismo erasmista.

Ninguna ciudad castellanoaragonesa contemporánea tuvo un mercado de ideas y de libros similar al constituido en el París de fines del XV y principios del XVI. Basta decir que, entre 1509 y 1514, años de permanencia del valenciano en esa ciudad, se imprimieron ahí no menos de 1421 libros, mientras que en Salamanca y Valencia, ciudades universitarias ambas, no queda constancia de más de 38 en cada una. Alcalá, con su orla de humanismo, no habría pasado de 23[78]. Y ya que de humanismo se trata, el propio Vives señaló a Juan de Vergara en

1527, con cierto tono polémico[79], que en aquella España no existían en abundancia los tres elementos indispensables para la fragua de un medio humanístico: eruditos dados al cultivo de la filología, abundancia de libros sobre esa materia, e impresores que difundieran por toda la península a los autores clásicos. Es cierto que Vives, si en vez de marchar a París en 1509, hubiese optado por Alcalá, aún habría alcanzado ahí el magisterio del anciano Nebrija. Con todo, el legado intelectual del valenciano resulta inimaginable sin un maestro de la talla e influencia de Erasmo, encontrado en los Países Bajos.

Aun si las relaciones personales entre Erasmo y Vives se agriaron considerablemente con el tiempo, el primero dejó una marca imprescindible en los aspectos medulares del pensamiento del segundo. Erasmista es la idea de la necesidad de nutrir la vida espiritual con oración interior, lectura del Nuevo Testamento y constante estudio, antes que con prácticas externas y reglas eclesiásticas; o que valía más el contacto directo con la fuerza vivificante de la palabra divina que no la discusión escolar de los dogmas de la iglesia. En vano se buscarán tales conceptos en sus escritos juveniles parisienses. Es cierto que en ellos se encuentra ya la preocupación vivesiana por la reforma sistemática de las disciplinas, que no es tan evidente en Erasmo. Pero al lado de él, Vives se afirmó en la confianza – compartida también por el humanismo italiano – en el papel regenerador de la educación, de la *doctrina*, y más aún, de aquella educación fundada en el estudio de las humanidades. Hay también ecos del roterodamo en el disgusto por los frailes – que el valenciano manifestó públicamente y en cartas privadas –, a los ques veía como encarnación de la religiosidad fundada en la tiranía de las prácticas externas, sin vida interior, así como de la más intolerante ignorancia, aunada a ociosidad. Por fin, es erasmista la convicción de que la fuente de todo bien en el seno de las sociedades es la paz. Una ética, por tanto, meditada desde el punto de vista de los ciu-

---

78. Para París, ver B. Moreau, *Inventaire Chronologique des Éditions Parisiennes du XVIe*, París, t. I (1501-1510); t. II (1511-1520), 1977. Para las tres ciudades universitarias peninsulares, F.J. Norton, *A descriptive Catalogue of Printing in Spain and Portugal. 1501-1520*, Cambridge University Press, 1978. Asimismo, J. Martín Abad, *La imprenta en Alcalá de Henares (1502-1600)*, Madrid, Arco Libros, 1991, 3 vols.; y L. Ruiz Fidalgo, *La imprenta en Salamanca (1501-1600)*, Madrid, Arco Libros, 1994, 3 vols.
79. La carta fue editada por A. Bonilla, en "Clarorum Hispaniensium…", pp. 266-267.

dadanos, de los burgueses, y no desde el de la casta nobiliaria, cuya tradicional función era la guerra.

Por tales motivos, carece de sentido la pregunta acerca de si Vives, en caso de haber permanecido en Valencia – y haber sobrevivido a la Inquisición – hubiera escrito ahí *De disciplinis*. Y más aún, sobre si lo hubiera hecho en latín o en romance. La pregunta es aún más ociosa en la medida que la totalidad de su obra escrita llegada hasta nosotros fue producida fuera de la patria. Y para seguir en la tierra baldía de las hipótesis, aun admitiendo la posibilidad de que, desde Valencia, hubiera logrado la misma formación literaria obtenida bajo sus maestros de París y Lovaina, queda la circunstancia de que Valencia y la propia península eran ya entonces una zona periférica del gran mercado del libro. En consecuencia, la obra escrita en la patria difícilmente habría tenido el grado de difusión europea que alcanzó[80]. En suma, aun admitiendo como probable que, de permanecer en Valencia, hubiera sido escritor, sin el exilio Vives no habría sido Vives. La patria lo impulsó al destierro, y éste lo hizo intelectual. "España me engendró – llegó a decir – y Francia me nutrió"[81].

Lo anterior no significa, para decirlo en términos de las polémicas de principios de este siglo, que Vives hubiese sido español sólo por el accidente de su nacimiento. Alejado física e intelectualmente de España, el infortunio de su familia y de varios de sus amigos humanistas lo obligó a mantenerse físicamente lejos, pero atento a lo que en ella sucedía. En ocasiones, como cuando se tradujo el *Enchiridio* al castellano, o durante las disputas teológicas de Valladolid de 1528 entre los partidarios y los enemigos de Erasmo, Vives se entusiasmó con la idea de una España convertida a su maestro[82]. Cuando trata de los frailes o de la represión inquisitorial, todo es despecho y pesimismo. A mi modo de ver, su experiencia personal como judeoconverso valenciano, perseguido y exiliado, da a su ideario político, fuertemente arraigado en el humanismo nórdico, un énfasis propio.

---

80. En "La lectura de Vives durante el Antiguo Régimen", que aparecerá en J. F. Alcina (Ed.), *Joan Lluís Vives i el seu temps*, Tarragona, Universitat de Tarragona, en prensa, creo haber demostrado que el impulso dado a la obra de Vives por las prensas de Basilea, a partir de 1536, fue determinante para su difusión a lo largo y ancho de Europa.

81. *De concordia et discordia*, l. III, en *I.L. Vivis Opera*, 1555, II, p. 805.

82. Es aún imprescindible, M. Bataillon, *Erasmo y España,* Trad. de Antonio Alatorre, México, FCE, 1966.

Ese acento es visible, primero, en su irreductible mentalidad urbana, "burguesa". Como ciudadano, experimentó en carne propia la indefensión que acarrean las épocas de discordia civil. Existe la protección de las leyes, pero su observancia se pulveriza donde irrumpe la violencia. Él, que aludió a su exilio como consecuencia de las disensiones civiles, desarrolló una idea central: en toda sociedad, todos, desde el más alto hasta el menor de sus componentes, son corresponsables de que la comunidad marche en concordia o en discordia. Esta última, en su opinión, arrastraba a la ruptura de los lazos que, en condiciones normales, ligaban a todos sus miembros. Pero semejante colapso no ocurría por azar, sino resultaba del mal comportamiento de todos. Análogamente, tampoco veía a la concordia a modo de ente abstracto o de don gratuito, sino como resultante de un concierto entre todos los miembros de la sociedad, por obra del cual cada uno aportaba lo propio, contribuyendo así al mejor cumplimiento de los fines conjuntos.

En consecuencia, ningún bien había de tenerse en más precio que la concordia, y ningún bien particular, ni siquiera el del príncipe, debía imponerse a costa del concierto social. La autoridad cumplía su función sólo si velaba por los intereses de la comunidad, y nunca, arrebatando lo propio de los súbditos. En una época en que los pensadores políticos buscaban organizar a la sociedad en torno al primado absoluto del monarca, el valenciano aparece como defensor, por así decir, de la sociedad civil, entendida como el interés general, en cuya conservación todos toman parte.

Asimismo, el acento vivista se aprecia en el tono personal, fruto de una experiencia vivida, y vivida dramáticamente, que lo llevó a un urgente llamado a aborrecer la discordia entre los príncipes, las religiones, los pueblos, y los miembros de una misma ciudad, en tanto que engendradora de una cadena de males concretos y tangibles; de ahí también su vehemente invitación a la concordia, origen y premisa de todos los bienes.

Congruente con esa convicción profunda, Joan Lluís Vives, que tantos atropellos sufrió en la persona de los suyos, y que más de una vez se expuso a ser denunciado por sus ideas, lejos de buscar venganza, en la que veía una práctica socialmente nociva, adoptó como lema personal: *sine querella*.

George Hugo Tucker

TO LOUVAIN AND ANTWERP, AND BEYOND :

THE CONTRASTING ITINERARIES OF DIOGO PIRES
(DIDACUS PYRRHUS LUSITANUS, 1517-99)
AND JOÃO RODRIGUES DE CASTELO BRANCO
(AMATUS LUSITANUS, 1511-68)

A. Diaspora: from Spain and Portugal to the Southern Low Countries, Italy and Beyond - Tricks of Perspective

Nullum tamen uitium hodie frequentius cernitur, gratius´que habetur, quàm impudentia in nostrorum Sacerdotum aula. crescit´que etiam illa in dies, & maior efficitur, quo plures habet, qui illàm fouent. Quid? quod magna accessio ad tale uitium facta est post, quàm patrum memoria in Italia constitutum est regnum Exterarum gentium, & in hanc Vrbem pulsi à suis Regibus concurrerunt ex ultima Hispania, quidam ementitum Christianorum nomen habentes, quos plebeia uoce Maranos dictitant. hi enim diuturna seruitute Regum Bethycorum, & aliorum Mauritanorum, qui usque ad nostram aetatem in Hispania regnarunt, ad nimiam sunt eruditi assentationem, quam perpetuam comitem impudentiae ueteres existimabant.

[Nowadays, in this court of our Priests, no vice is discerned more frequently or held more agreeable than shamelessness. It even grows by the day, becoming more pronounced the more people it has fostering it. Moreover, there has been a great increase in such vice ever since, within the memory of our fathers, there was established in Italy a whole realm of Foreign peoples, and, driven by their Kings from far-flung Spain, there flocked to this City [of Rome] persons who mendaciously bear the name of Christians and are commonly called 'Marranos'. These, by their long servitude under the Andalusian Kings and other Moors who reigned in Spain right up to our own time, have been schooled in excessive flattery, which the Ancients ever considered to be the perpetual companion of shamelessness.][1]

---

1. *Petri Alcyonii Medices Legatus de exsilio* (Venetiis, in aedibus Aldi et Andreae Asulani soceri, mense Novembri 1522), f. h1ro.

The date is 1512, and the setting the palace of the Medici in Rome. The words are spoken by Cardinal Giovanni de' Medici (soon to be Pope Leo X, 1513-22) to two fellow Florentine exiles and kinsmen, Giovanni's cousin Giulio de' Medici (the future Clement VII, 1523-34), and his nephew Lorenzo (later Duke of Urbino, 1516-19). In addition to blaming the moral 'shamelessness' of the Roman clergy upon the flattery of Sephardic Jewish immigrants from Spain masquerading in Italy as New Christians, Giovanni, in the same breath and in an equally bold telescoping of history, will also blame the former influence of the French in Avignon at the time the papal court was transferred there by Clement V at the beginning of the Fourteenth Century.

Or at least that is the picture painted *circa* 1521-22 by the Venetian-born humanist scholar, Petrus Alcyonius (1487-1527?), in the fiction of his Ciceronian dialogue 'on exile', *Medices Legatus de exsilio* (Venice, 1522) – a work whose most immediate purpose was to attract for its ambitious, humbly-born author the attention and patronage of Cardinal Giulio de' Medici, not quite yet Clement VII.

If we look at surviving copies of Alcyonius's dialogue, we can see that these remarks provoked much marginal comment from contemporary annotators – particularly in reaction to Giovanni's hostile, ideologically loaded and linguistically curious reference to 'Marani', in a Northern-Italian Latinization (with one 'r') of the Spanish vernacular term of abuse *marrano* (employed in preference to the discreeter, Greco-Latin term, *neophytus*, corresponding to the *neofito* of Italian vernacular usage).[2] Nowhere was reader-reaction more indignant at such arrant pro-Roman hypocrisy and chauvinism than in the margin of Paulus Manutius's own personal copy now in the Vatican. There, the annotator, writing in the late 1540s, blames the disintegration of the authority of the Roman Catholic Church and 'the Christian name' (in the face of the German Protestant, Anglican and Gallican Reforms) rather upon the shamelessly corrupt and ambitious Italians and Romans themselves. 'Would that your race had never existed!...', he writes, 'Would that the Vatican had lacked such monsters!...', he

---

2. See G.H. Tucker, 'Exile exiled : Petrus Alcyonius (1487-1527?) in a travelling-chest' (in particular, n. 48), in *States of Exile and Displacement in Neo-Latin Writings of the Renaissance*, Acts of a day-conference organized by G.H. Tucker, in *Journal of the Institute of Romance Studies* 2 (1993) 83-190 (pp. 83-103). I am grateful to Dr Martin Maiden for the perception that the single 'r' in 'Marani' reflects Northern Italian vernacular usage.

exclaims, implicitly rejecting Giovanni de' Medici's use of both French courtiers in Avignon and Sephardic Iberian Jews in Italy as historical scapegoats; indeed, he echoes the sentiments of Leo X's successor, the Dutch reforming pope Hadrian VI (1522-23), who in dealing with the Lutheran revolt in Germany, blamed the disorder of the Church upon the Curia itself.[3] Nonetheless, it is quite surprising that the near-contemporary annotator, accepts as historically accurate the chauvinistic sentiments attributed by the author Alcyonius to the future Leo X in his fictional conversation of 1512 with the future Clement VII.

These xenophobic sentiments probably reflect the obsessive pro-Roman patriotism and cultural ambitions of their author, the non-Roman *outsider* Alcyonius himself, more than they do the actual policies of Leo X and Clement VII with regard to the Jews in Italy.[4] True to their family's traditional tolerance of Jews in Florence, these two Medici popes tended rather to attempt to protect Iberian judaizing New Christians from the jurisdiction of the Inquisition in Spain and Portugal as well as in the Papal State – on the grounds, principally, of their enforced (and thus arguably invalid) general 'conversion' by King Manoel I ('the Fortunate', 1495-1521) of Portugal in 1497.[5] This papal

---

3. Roma Bibl. Apost. Vat. Aldine II.27 (f. h1ro, righthand margin), in full: 'magna tu hunc hominem / urges censura. utinam / genus tuum numquam exstitisset. / non Germaniam, non Britanniam, / non Franciam, cum universo fere / aquilone amisissemus. omne / malum, omnes clades, vestri / generis ignavia, libidine, / ambitione, <?>inscitia, / avaritiaque sunt importata / Christiano nomini. utinam / Vaticanum talibus monstris / caruisset. satis vestro scelere / poenarum dedimus vel / diis, hominibus ve. / faxint numina, tuentia / Romanis ut sufficiant, / neu posthac nostro cruore / vestra piacula eluantur. [You greatly censure this man [Clement V]. Would that your race had never existed! And that we had not lost Germany, nor Britain, nor France, together with virtually the whole North! All the evil, all the disasters, have, through the cowardliness, lust, ambition, ignorance (?), and greed of your race, been brought upon the Christian name. Would that the Vatican had lacked such monsters! We have paid enough penalties for your wickedness to both the gods and men. May the deities who watch [over us] bring it to pass that these suffice the Romans, and that henceforth your sins are not washed in our blood.]'. On Hadrian VI's not dissimilar position at the diet of Nuremburg (December, 1522), see 'Hadrian VI', in J.N.D. Kelley, *The Oxford Dictionary of the Popes* (Oxford, 1986), pp. 258-9.

4. See Tucker, 'Exile exiled', *passim* .

5. Cf. C. Roth, *A History of the Marranos*, Jewish Publication Society of America (Philadelphia / London, 1932), p. 83; B. Pullan, *The Jews of Europe and the Inquisition of Venice 1550-1670* (Oxford, 1983), pp. 173-4; J. Edwards, *The Jews in Christian Europe 1400-1700* (London / New York, 1988; paperback edn. 1991), p. 78; J.-P. Filippini, 'L'État pontifical', in *Les Juifs d'Espagne : histoire d'une diaspora 1492-1992*, ouvrage dirigé par H. Méchoulan, préface d'E. Morin, Librairie européenne des idées (Paris, 1992), pp. 304-5 (p. 304).

display of sympathy was in diametric opposition to the anti-Jewish, pro-Inquisitorial, pressures usually applied by the Emperor Charles V in conjunction with John III of Portugal.[6] If in Rome Leo tolerated, indeed cultivated, the presence of Jewish refugees from the Inquisition, Clement, like his immediate successors, Paul III and Julius III, no less fostered for trade purposes the Jewish mercantile community of papal Ancona. Indeed, further testimonies to the Medici papal tolerance include, notoriously, Clement's protection in 1530 of the Portuguese Jewish Messianic prophet Solomon Molcho (also known as Diogo Pires) from the Inquisition (again in stark contrast with Charles V); perhaps most famously of all, Clement issued his *Bull of Pardon* (April 7, 1533) protecting the wayward, so-called New Christians.[7]

Alcyonius's slanted presentation of recent papal history also conjures up the image of a more distant Age of Jewish courtly influence in Southern Muslim Spain in the Eleventh and Twelfth Centuries – a heyday (crabbedly described as 'servitude') which he extends right up to the fall of Granada in 1492, using this historical exaggeration as a justification for an alarmist claim about contemporary Jewish influence in the papal court. However, any mention of the crucial role of Portugal after the Spanish expulsion of the Jews in 1492 is suppressed, allowing the author to ignore the contestable issue of the forced General Conversion of Portuguese and Spanish Jews in Lisbon five years later (1497), after these had generally failed to convert of their own accord under the threat of Manoel I's initial expulsion order of December 5, 1496. Indeed, the author thus also sidesteps the related matter of Manoel's subsequent prevention by royal decree (April 20, 1499) of even the

---

6. See Roth, *A History of the Marranos,* pp. 71, 83; S.W. Baron, *A Social and Religious History of the Jews,* The Jewish Publication Society of America, 18 vols (Philadelphia / New York / London, 1952-83), XIII - *Inquisition, Renaissance, and Reformation* (1969), pp. 52, 91-2; J. Israel, *European Jewry in the Age of Mercantilism 1550-1750,* second revised edn. (Oxford, 1989), p. 16.

7. See A. Milano, *Storia degli ebrei in Italia* (Torino, 1963), pp. 238-42; Baron, *A Social and Religious History,* XIII, 103-15; Filippini, 'L'État Pontifical', p. 304. On the Messianic Solomon Molcho, cf., in addition, H. Beinart, '*Ch. 4* : The Conversos and their Fate', and M. Idel, '*Ch. 5* : Religion, Thought and Attitudes: the Impact of the Expulsion on the Jews', in *Spain and the Jews:* The Sephardi Experience *1492 and After,* ed. E. Kedourie (London, 1992), pp. 92-122 (p. 117), and pp. 123-39 (p. 136), respectively.

emigration of these so-called New Christians (except by royal license), lest they revert to Judaism elsewhere.[8]

This in fact brings us to one of the more significant aspects of Alcyonius's exile dialogue, which is as antipathetic to the external realities of Sephardic Jewish exile, as it is contradicted internally by its own Stoicizing protestations that the earth is the common 'patria' of all.[9] The dialogue's fictional date of 1512 and its compositional date of 1521 constitute two symbolic moments in the dramatic peripeteia of the Marrano story – that is, in the judaizing New Christians' attempts at emigration and flight from Portugal, often to embark as much on a spiritual, as on a geographical, cultural or mercantile, itinerary: via England and the Southern Low Countries initially, to the states of Italy, and thence on to the Dalmatian coast and the religious freedoms enjoyed (at least to begin with) in the Ottoman Empire, in what was at once a progressive journey towards a re-establishment, or (for those of the post-Conversion generation) a re-discovery, of a Jewish identity.[10] The first (fictional) date, 1512, marks the first renewal of the Manoel I's edict of March 1 1507 finally granting permission to New Christians to emigrate after the horrors of the Lisbon massacre of April 1506.[11] The second (compositional) date, 1521, marks not just the end of Manoel I's reign and the beginning of John III's (1521-57), which was to introduce the Inquisition into Portugal, but also the re-imposition by

---

8. See J. Mendes dos Remedios, *Os Judeus em Portugal*, 2 vols (Coimbra, 1895-1928), I (1895), pp. 284-303; Roth, *A History of the Marranos*, 55-64; Baron, *A Social and Religious History*, XIII, 44-6; Pullan, *The Jews of Europe*, pp. 201-2; Edwards, *The Jews*, pp. 37-8; A. Novinsky, 'Juifs et nouveaux chrétiens du Portugal', in Méchoulan (ed.), *Les Juifs d'Espagne*, pp. 53-107 (pp. 80-3).

9. See Tucker, 'Exile exiled', *passim* (and nn. 49-50).

10. The classic Marrano journey; cf. Pullan, *The Jews of Europe*, pp. 172, 211-3. On the initial Sephardic commercial elite in Antwerp (as opposed to the community later settled in Amsterdam), and on the changing fortunes of Sephardic Jews among the Turks (even in the course of just the Sixteenth Century), cf. also J. Israel, '*Ch. 8* : The Sephardim in the Netherlands', and A. Rodrigue, '*Ch. 7* : The Sephardim in the Ottoman Empire', in Kedourie (ed.), *Spain and the Jews*, pp. 189-212 (pp. 189-92), and pp. 162-88 (pp. 162-80), respectively.

11. On the massacre and Manoel's subsequent edicts see Mendes dos Remedios, *Os Judeus*, I, 306-21; Roth, *A History of the Marranos*, pp. 64-6; Baron, *A Social and Religious History*, XIII, 46-7; Y.H. Yerushalmi, *The Lisbon Massacre of 1506 and the Royal Image in the Shebet Yehudah*, Hebrew Union College Annual Supplements 1 (Cincinnati, 1976), *passim* (pp. 87-9 for the text of the 1507 edict permitting emigration).

that new King of emigration restrictions upon the New Christians, in a desperate attempt to close the flood-gates upon the veritable tide of their exodus.[12]

In short, Alcyonius's exile dialogue is remarkable for studiously concealing the precise demographic factor that most immediately motivates its anti-semitism: the Marrano emigrations from Portugal from 1507 onwards.

By contrast, the aim of this study is to investigate the nature of that Portuguese Jewish migration to the Southern Low Countries and beyond by exploring, principally, the complementary cases of two celebrated figures of the post-General Conversion, post-1497, generation of so-called New Christians: the humanist student, scholar and poet, Didacus Pyrrhus Lusitanus (1517-99), otherwise known as Jacobus Flavius Eborensis, or Diogo Pires; and the celebrated physician and commentator on Dioscorides, João Rodrigues de Castelo Branco (1511-68), more usually known as Amatus Lusitanus.[13]

I shall begin by focusing upon their presence, cultural contacts and various relations in Louvain and Antwerp in the mid-to-late-1530s. However, I shall also endeavour (perhaps more importantly) to demonstrate the contrasting ways in which they lived their outwardly similar, spiritual, intellectual, and geographical itineraries to Louvain and Antwerp, *and beyond* (principally, to Ferrara, Ancona, Dalmatian Ragusa, and Ottoman Thessalonika). By so doing, I hope to illustrate – at least

---

12. See Mendes dos Remedios, *Os Judeus,* II - *Vicissitudes da sua historia desde a época em que foram expulsos até à extinção da Inquisição* (1928), pp. 47-52; Roth, *A History of the Marranos,* pp. 66-73; Novinsky, 'Juifs et nouveaux chrétiens', p. 85; R.G. Fuks-Mansfeld, 'Les Nouveaux chrétiens à Anvers aux XVIe et XVIIe siècles', in Méchoulan (ed.), *Les Juifs d'Espagne,* pp. 183-90 (pp. 183-5).

13. For most recent discussion of both these figures, and their works, cf. G.H. Tucker, 'Didacus Pyrrhus Lusitanus (1517-99), Poet of Exile', *Humanistica Lovaniensia: Journal of Neo-Latin Studies* XLI (1992), 175-98 (pp. 189-98 listing chronologically Didacus Pyrrhus's published and unpublished works and their present location in European libraries); C. Ascenso André, 'Diogo Pires: um símbolo na Diáspora Lusitana', in [Acts of] *Associação Internacional de Lusitanistas* (Poitiers, 1988), 49-63; id., 'Diogo Pires e a lembrança de Erasmo', *Humanitas* (1990), 81-98; id., *Mal de Ausência: o canto do exílio na lírica do humanismo português* (Coimbra, 1992), pp. 391-436; M. Santoro, *Amato Lusitano ed Ancona,* Textos Humanísticos Portugueses 8 (Coimbra, 1991). Cf. also M. Lemos, *Amato Lusitano: a sua vida e a sua opera* (Porto, 1907); J. Taditch, *Jevreji u Dubrovniku do polovine XVII stoljetcha* (Sarajevo, 1937), pp. 275-97 ('Amatus Lusitanus'), 298-314 ('Didak Pir').

to some degree – the complex range of contradictions, ambiguities and strategies within the Marrano condition itself – a complexity and a variety certainly ignored by the prejudiced Petrus Alcyonius's dialogue *De exsilio*, but which has been recognized as fundamental by recent historians of early-modern Marranism: for example, Yosef Yerushalmi, on the Spanish physician Fernando (later Jitzhaq) Cardoso (1603/4?-1683); Brian Pullan, on Marrano victims of the Venetian Inquisition (1550-1670); and Yirmiyahu Yovel on the Iberian-Jewish Dutch philosopher Baruch Spinoza (1632-77).[14]

This Marrano complexity and variety no less deserves our attention today; in the earlier cases of Diogo Pires and João Rodrigues – as in those of several of their Marrano contemporaries – Louvain and Antwerp, like Ferrara later, represent but the initial stages in a more fundamental journey of inner exile, which may unfold in different ways.[15] It is only on Diogo Pires's death in the ghetto of Ragusa (Dubrovnik) in 1599, that we shall find any written indication of his true Jewish name: Isaia Cohen – a name he would also have used privately among the Iberian Jewish community of Ferrara in the 1540s to the mid-1550s. By contrast, when João Rodrigues de Castelo Branco publicly styles himself 'Amatus Lusitanus' in his writings and professional life in Italy, he is already giving a subtle indication of the Jewish name 'Chaviv' by which he will later be known in Ottoman Thessalonika, where he died in 1568.[16]

---

14. Y.H. Yerushalmi, *Dalla corte al ghetto: La vita, le opere, le peregrinazioni del marrano Cardoso nell' Europa del Seicento*, presentazione di M. Luzzati e M. Olivari, introduzione di S.W. Baron, transl. M. Sumbulovich (revised by A. Mottola) [from the English *From Spanish Court to Italian Ghetto Isaac Cardoso: A Study in Seventeenth-Century Marranism and Jewish Apologetics* (1971; 1981)], Garzanti: Collezione storica (Milano, 1991), pp. 33-71; Pullan, *The Jews of Europe*, pp. 201-42; Y. Yovel, *Spinoza and Other Heretics*, 2 vols (Princeton, New Jersey, 1989), I - *The Marrano of Reason*, pp. 15-39.

15. Cf. Yovel, *Spinoza*, I, 22-4, and Idel, 'Religion, Thought and Attitudes', pp. 135-36.

16. On Didacus's Jewish name (and his immediate family's names), see Taditch, *Jevreji*, pp. 302, 307; J.P. Santos Carvalho, 'De Évora a Ragusa: a peregrinação sem regresso de Didacus Pyrrhus Lusitanus', *O Instituto* 140-41 (1980-1), 79-100 (pp. 91-2); A. da Costa Ramalho, 'Didacus Pyrrhus Lusitanus, Poeta e Humanista', *Humanitas* 35-6 (1983-4), 1-17 (pp. 16-17); Tucker, 'Didacus Pyrrhus Lusitanus', pp. 175, 182 (n. 14), 183-4 (n. 20). On Amatus's, see V. Colorni, *Judaica Minora: Saggi sulla storia dell' ebraismo italiano dall' antichità all' età moderna*, Pubblicazioni della Facoltà Giuridica dell' Università di Ferrara (serie seconda) 14 (Milano, 1983), p. 721.

B. Diogo Pires and João Rodrigues de Castelo Branco in Louvain and Antwerp circa 1535-40, and the Marrano Itinerary of Exile

Diogo Pires – or Didacus Pyrrhus – records the date of his departure from his native land, under the orders of his father, as 1535, in a prose gloss that accompanies his late-published Latin epitaph on John III of Portugal. Moreover, through a close textual echo this gloss implicitly equates its author with Virgil's landless outcast of the *Eclogues*, Meliboeus:

Ioannes III.

Rex, quo nemo magis populum dilexit, & in quem
   Non potuit populi crescere maior amor.

Sub hoc rege iussu patris, adolescens vixdum xiix. annum egressus, id quod non sine lachrymis scribo. Et patriae fines, & dulcia rura reliqui.   an. 1535.

[John III.

A King, more than whom no one loved his people, and for
   Whom his people's love could not grow greater.

Under this king, at my father's bidding, when a youth barely in my eighteenth year – not without tears do I write this – 'I forsook the confines and sweet fields of my fatherland' in the year 1535.]

(Diogo Pires, *Cato Minor* (Venice, 1592; 1596))[17]

The function of the exiled author's poignant gloss is in fact cleverly ambiguous, highlighting also the epitaph's potential for a savagely ironic reading – but only for those few privy to the unstated, religious reasons behind the father's otherwise seemingly arbitrary order to depart.

The year 1535, recorded in the gloss, was indeed an ominous one for Portuguese New Christians; John III's original 1521 prohibition of

---

17. *Flavii Iacobi Eborensis Cato Minor, sive Disticha Moralia Ad Ludi magistros Olysipponenses. Accessere epigrammata, & alia nonnulla eodem auctore,... Opus pium, et erudiendis pueris adprimè necessarium. ...*, 2nd augmented edn. (Venetiis, apud Felicem Valgrisium, 1596) [Évora, Bibl. Pública Res. 6054; Lisbon, Bibl. Ajuda 64-II-26], p. 76; text with error (*xii-* for 'xiix.') also in 1st edn. (Venetiis, sub signum Leonis, 1592) [Bergamo, Cibl. Civ. Ciquecentine 1,620; Roma, Bibl. Ang. [ss]-10-58; Venezia, Bibl. Marc. 221.c.135], p. 123. The allusion is to Virgil, *Eclogues*, 1.3 (Meliboeus to Tityrus: 'nos patriae finis et dulcia linquimus arva').

their emigration was then renewed for a second time (after its initial three-year renewal in 1532).[18] Moreover, following Charles V's successful attack on Muslim Tunis (and upon the refugee Iberian Jews there) in1535-6, Pope Paul III, unable to resist Imperial pressure, was about to repeal, in 1536, Clement VII's *Bull of Pardon* (of 1533) protecting New Christians from the jurisdiction of the Inquisition (whose introduction into Portugal had already been secretly agreed with the King in 1531).[19] Didacus's father seems, therefore, to have acted not a moment too soon, and possibly illegally.

Didacus's resultant departure, to study at Louvain, was a hasty and disruptive affair, following hard upon the eighteen-year-old's return from studies (in Dialectics and Rhetoric) across the border in Salamanca, under Charles V's confessor, Dominico de Soto (1494-1560) and Fernando Nuñez 'Pintianus' (*circa* 1473-1553).[20] We gather this from a poem, in which the departing Didacus bids farewell to his kinsman and friend, João Rodrigues, the future 'Amatus', who just five years previously had graduated in medicine from the same University of Salamanca :[21]

Ad Ioannem Rodericum medicum Louanium petiturus.

Quos patimur cassus, & quos Roderice labores,

Quae ue pericla uides.

Dum sequimur toto fugientes orbe puellas

A Ioue progenitas.

---

18. Roth, *A History of the Marranos*, p. 196.

19. See Roth, *A History of the Marranos*, pp. 68-71; on Charles V's African campaign, and its consequences for the Jewish community in Tunis, cf. also M. Abitbol, 'Juifs ibériques, musulmans et chrétiens après l'expulsion: le cas nord-africain', in *Les Juifs d'Espagne*, pp. 519-22 (p. 519).

20. On 'F. Nuñez Pintianus', cf. Lemos, *Amato Lusitano*, p. 21. D. Körbler, 'Život i rad humanista Didaka Portugalca, napose u Dubrovniku', *Rad Jugoslavenske Akademije Znanosti i Umjetnosti*, knjiga 216, Razreda Historičko-Filologičkoga 94 (Zagreb, 1917), pp. 1-169 (p. 162), identifies Didacus's other teacher at Salamanca, 'Sotus', with *Dominico* de Soto, born in Segovia – an identification borne out by the fact that in both editions of his *Cato Minor* Didacus placed a 'Scholium' telling of his former teacher between his epigrams on the towns of 'Secobia' (addressed to 'Sote pater') and 'Salamanca': 'Sotus è Prædicatoria familia, olim præceptor meus, in Dialecticis, diuinarum literarum scientia Hispaniam illustrauit' ((1592), p. 125 ; (1596), p. 78 [with corrections, as quoted here]).

21. See Lemos, *Amato Lusitano*, pp. 10, 39; Milano, *Storia degli ebrei*, p. 632; Tucker, 'Didacus Pyrrhus Lusitanus', p. 177 (n. 5).

En ego qui dudum votis petii omnibus vndas
   Tormidis aureolas.
Rursus in ire fretum, rursus candentia cogor
   Pandere vela noto.
Vela noto, & toties iactatam credere vitam
   Fluctibus Hesperiis.
Heu patrias vnquam dabitur ne reuisere sedes, ... ?
Interea longum veteris Roderice sodalis
   Viue vale'que memor. ...

[**To João Rodrigues, physician, on setting out for Louvain.**
What misfortunes, and what travails we suffer, Rodrigues,
   Or what perils, you well see,
As long as we pursue throughout the whole world those fleeing girls
   Born of Jupiter.
Behold, I who but a while ago sought with all my prayers the golden
   Waters of the Tormes,
Am again compelled to go out to sea, again to spread
   White sails to the South Wind,
Sails to the South Wind, and to entrust a life so often storm-tossed
   To the Western waves.
Alas, will it ever be granted me to go back to my native home, ... ?
Meanwhile, Rodrigues, of your old companion ever mindful,
   Live long and fare well. ...]
               (Diogo Pires, *Carmina* (Ferrara, 1545))[22]

22. Vv. 1-11, 27-8 (of 32 vv.), in *Didaci Pyrrhi Lusitani Carminum liber unus* (Ferrariae, apud Franciscum Rubrium, 1545), ff. G3vo-4ro. Cf. A. da Costa Ramalho, *Estudos sobre a época do Rinascimento* (Coimbra, 1969), pp. 187-95 ['XIII - A propósito do "Amato Lusitano" de Ricardo Jorge'] (pp. 189-92), for text and translation with contemporary glosses on Salamanca's river Tormes; cf. also Ascenso André, *Mal de Ausência*, pp. 422-23. On Diogo Pires's time at the University of Salamanca, see Santos Carvalho, 'De Évora a Ragusa', p. 83; Körbler, 'Život i rad humanista', p. 162.

Before setting off from Lisbon, then, Didacus had paused poetically to share his nostalgia for Salamanca's river Tormes with the fellow ex-alumnus, João Rodrigues. Later, he would again evoke the Tormes of his early student days in an epistolary poem from Ferrara addressed to his nephew then studying letters at Salamanca University, one Didacus Vassaeus (Diogo Vaz / of Viseu?), the son of a brother or sister who had remained behind.[23]

As for João Rodrigues – or Amatus –, it was the pressing political and religious circumstances of 1535, rather than the fancied pursuit of the Muses to university towns throughout the world, that soon impelled him as well to spread sail for what was to become as it were their common voyage to Byzantium. Not only would Didacus's and Amatus's dates in the Low Countries coincide, but so also would their long subsequent presence in Italy (particularly in Ferrara and Ancona) in the 1540s and early 1550s, before their further flight to Ragusa and Constantinople – the one finally settling in that Catholic Adriatic republic of St Blasius (Ragusa), and the other ending his long journey of exile in Ottoman Thessalonika.[24] From Ragusa, the ultimate survivor of the pair, Didacus, would pause once again, to bid a poetic farewell to his companion Amatus, in a moving epitaph that was also a tribute to his friend's famed medical skills:

Amati Lusitani medici Physici praestantissimi Epit.
obiit fere sexagenarius pestilentia Thessalonicae
ann. 1568.

Qui toties fugientem animam sistebat in aegro,

    Corpore, Letheis aut reuocabat aquis,

Gratus ob id populis, & magnis regibus aequè,

    Hic iacet, hanc moriens pressit Amatus humum. ...

[Epitaph of Amatus Lusitanus most excellent medical Physician.
He died, almost sixty years old, from the plague in Thessalonika,
in the year 1568.

He who so often would detain the fleeing soul in the ailing

    Body, or summon it back from Lethe's waters,

---

23. Diogo Pires, 'Didaco Vassaeo nepoti suo qui Salamancae litteris dat operam', vv. 56-68, in *D.P.L. Carminum lib.* (1545), ff. C4ro-D3ro (f. D1vo). On an anonymous brother left behind in Portugal, cf. Tucker, 'Didacus Pyrrhus Lusitanus', p. 182 (n. 14).

24. See Tucker, 'Didacus Pyrrhus Lusitanus, *passim* .

Dear, on that account, to peoples, and to great kings, equally,

Lies here, in death Amatus lies upon this soil. ...]

(Diogo Pires, *Cato Minor* (1592; 1596))[25]

Let us return, however, to the beginning of their journey – as it was seen, moreover, by Didacus himself, from his earlier point of hindsight in the Ferrara of the mid-1540s.

In a an elegant Latin letter to the contemporary historian, Paolo Giovio, written from Ferrara in February 1547, Didacus sketched out, with bold frankness and great lucidity, the whole Spanish-Portuguese, Papal-Imperial history of his and his family's emigration from Portugal as so-called 'Neophyti' (a term about which he ironizes). In the letter, he also shows a familiarity with London as a place of refuge for Marranos, on a par with Antwerp, and he even maintains that he has personally witnessed a pledge of welcome and protection given at court by Henry VIII himself.[26] This letter thus also incidentally testifies to Didacus and his family's temporary halt in England on their way to the Low Countries (and thence to Italy) – as is later corroborated by the testimony of Lilio Gregorio Giraldi, in his presentation of Didacus Pyrrhus as a character in his famous *Dialogi duo de poetis nostrorum temporum* (Florence, 1551), a work fictionally set in Ferrara, to which Didacus also contributed poetically. In the *Dialogi*, Giraldi pretends to make use of the well-travelled Pyrrhus's acquaintance with English, as well as with Iberian, humanism.[27] As we know, it was not unusual for Iberian New Christians to halt temporarily in England, in order to ascertain whether or when it was safe to carry on by ship to the Imperial-controlled Low Countries. Indeed, in the year of Didacus's departure, 1535, no less a personage than the newly-widowed Gracia

---

25. Vv. 1-4 (of 8 vv.), in *F.I.E. Cato Minor* (1596), p. 215; also in 1st edn. (1592), p. 145.

26. 'Didacus Pyrrhus Paulo Iovio S.D.', in MS Modena Bibl. Est., est. lat. 174, ff. 161ro-162vo. The whole story of the establishment of the Inquisition in Spain and in Portugal, and of the roles of Manoel I, John III, the latter's wife and Charles V, in the forced conversion of the Jews in Portugal, their persecution as New Christians and their emigration to the *relative* safety of London and Antwerp, is there recounted as background to the story of Didacus and his family's equally sudden subsequent emigration from the Low Countries to Italy, again at his father's behest. Cf. Tucker, 'Didacus Pyrrhus Lusitanus', pp. 182-3 (and n. 18).

27. Cf. Tucker, 'Didacus Pyrrhus Lusitanus', p. 180; Tucker, 'Exile exiled', p. 91.

Mendes (Beatrix de Luna), of the great Marrano merchant family, took the same route as the Pires family, stopping in England on her way to join her brother-in-law Diogo Mendes in Antwerp; she also took with her her whole family, including her young nephew and future son-in-law João Miguez (later to be known in the Ottoman Empire as Joseph Nasi, duke of Naxos), who, whilst a young man in the Low Countries, was to matriculate in the University of Louvain on September 1, 1542.[28]

In their train also travelled to the Southern Low Countries João Miguez's Marrano Tutor in Portugal, the Spanish-born writer and poet, Alonso Núñez de Reinoso (*circa* 1492- ?), whose pastoral novel *Clareo y Florisea* – published by Giolito de' Ferrari in Venice at the beginning of 1552, and dedicated to the same João Miguez – has been interpreted by some as a discreet allegory of the Iberian Jews' exile and the ambiguities of their *converso* status.[29] After a controversial period in Venice (*circa* 1545-50), Núñez and his patrons, the Mendes-Nasi family – like Didacus and Amatus before them – would eventually progress to Ferrara at the beginning of the 1550s, where Núñez saw the publication in 1554 of another, potentially allegorical, Iberian pastoral romance, the *Menina e moça* of his late Portuguese friend and fellow *converso*, Bernardim Ribeiro (1482? - ?); it was probably Núñez who delivered Ribeiro's manuscript to Abraham Usque's Jewish press in Ferrara, which was sponsored by Gracia Mendes herself (now known as Gracia Nasi) – indeed, just as already in the Low Countries, Núñez is credited by some with having delivered the manuscript of another romance by Ribeiro for publication by the Martin Nutius press in Antwerp in 1545.[30] By virtue of their common Ferrara connection through Núñez,

28. See C. Roth, *A History of the Jews in England* (Oxford, 1941), pp. 136-7; Roth, *A History of the Marranos*, p. 253. On the date of Miguez's enrolment in Louvain, see C.H. Rose, *Alonso Núñez de Reinoso: The Lament of a Sixteenth-Century Exile* (Fairleigh Dickinson University Press: Rutherford / Madison / Teaneck, 1971), p. 49 (n. 60).

29. *La historia de los amores de Clareo y Florisea y de los trabajos de la sin ventura Isea* (Venezia, Gabriel Giolito de Ferrari, [January] 1552), for discussion of which, as an exile allegory, and in further relation to Bernardim Ribeiro, Ortensio Landi, Samuel Usque, and the Mendes-Nasi family, see Rose, *Alonso Núñez,* pp. 9-164.

30. The poem 'Ao longo de hua ribeira / que vay polo pee da serra', whose attribution to Ribeiro has been questioned; see Rose, *Alonso Núñez*, pp. 49-50 (and n. 62), and pp. 54-60 on the Mendes-Nasis' period in Venice and move to Ferrara. Cf. Pullan, *The Jews of Europe*, pp. 176-7, and R. Bonfil, 'Ferrare: un port sûr et paisible pour la diaspora séfarade', in *Les Juifs d'Espagne*, pp. 295-303 (pp. 298-300).

their shared Marrano heritage and their similar pastoral form, both Ribeiro's *Menina e moça* and Núñez's *Clareo y Florisea* are circumstantially linked, as well as historically and generically related, to Samuel Usque's famous three books of pastoral dialogues entitled *Consolaçam ás Tribulaçoens de Ysrael*, which were also published by the Abraham Usque press at Ferrara on September 7, 1553, and dedicated to Gracia Nasi (a second edition appearing almost immediately in Amsterdam, on September 27).[31]

All three works, centring in their different ways on the Jewish community of Ferrara, would presumably have been known in Italy to Didacus Pyrrhus and Amatus Lusitanus; indeed, these two men, like Gracia Mendes-Nasi, had shared in the events that led to their publication, when they participated in the historical migration that took Núñez de Reinoso and the Mendes family to Antwerp *circa* 1535. Perhaps it is no coincidence, then, that Didacus had likened his banished self of that moment to that classic figure of pastoral exile – the displaced Meliboeus of Virgil's first eclogue. It should be added that the appearance of these three Iberian pastoral works coincided as well with the highpoint of Ferrarese Iberian-Jewish culture and of its printing press, which in March 1553 saw the production, notably, of Abraham Usque's Old Testament in Spanish (translated from the Hebrew), for both Christian and Jewish usage[32] – or again, which in 1556 saw the re-publication in Hebrew of the great *Itinerary* of the twelfth-century Spanish Jew, Benjamin of Tudela (Navarra), following the first Hebrew edition

---

31. Links discussed by Rose, *Alonso Núñez*, *passim*, and more recently explored by B. Damiani and B. Mujica, *Et in Arcadia Ego: Essays on Death in the Pastoral Novel* (University Press of America: Lanham / New York / London, 1990), pp. 18-46 (Ch. 2: 'The Last Hour: Bernardim Ribeiro's Menina e Moça'). For Samuel Usque's text and editorial discussion of its two original editions, see Samuel Usque, *Consolaçam ás Tribulaçoens de Israel.* ..., ed. J. Mendes dos Remedios, Subsidios para o estudo da Historia da Litteratura Portuguesa 8-10, 3 vols (Coimbra, 1906-7). See also Isabel de Sena, 'Voices and Disguises in the Sentimental Romance: Bernardim Ribeiro's *Menina e moça*', *Journal of the Institute of Romance Studies* [University of London] 3 (1994-5), 129-96 (pp. 138, 141).

32. *Biblia en lengua Española* (Ferrara, con yndustria y deligencia de Duarte Pinel Portugues, a costa y despesa de Jeronimo de Vargas Español, 1 Março 1553) [Christian version, dedicated to the Duke of Ferrara; Adams B1254]; (Ferrara, con yndustria y deligencia de Abraham Vsque Portugues, a costa y despesa de yom Tob Atias hijo de Leui Atias, 14 Adar 5313) [Jewish version; Adams B1255].

of Constantinople 1543, and long preceding the first Latin edition of Antwerp 1575.[33]

Nor should we lose from sight the political background to the arrival of the Pires and Mendes households in the Southern Low Countries, which coincided with a particularly difficult time for would-be New Christian emigrants thither. It was in the aftermath of the notorious arrests and (failed) trial in Antwerp three years previously (1531-2) of Diogo Mendes (and of other Iberian Marrano merchants) for judaizing, for acting for Jews in the Ottoman Empire, and for monopolizing the lucrative spice trade. It also followed Charles V's ban of the same year, 1532, prohibiting admittance to the Low Countries of New Christians migrating to Turkey. Yet it was prior to the release, in 1536, of Mendes's international agent, António Fernandez, as well as before Charles V's grant of permission to New Christians in 1537 to settle in Antwerp with full rights.[34]

Now, if the modern historian of Erasmus's Collegium Trilingue in Louvain, Henry de Vocht, associated Didacus Pyrrhus with the 'Pirez, or Piris, family, Portuguese merchants who had settled at Antwerp', he also identified the date of his matriculation in Louvain (under the name of 'Jacobus Pyrrus Lusitanus') as January 28 1536 – a date with which Luís de Matos, chronicling the Portuguese presence in the University of Paris, concurred, further pointing out that Didacus, in his 1547 letter to Giovio, also revealed that during the period of his family's presence in Antwerp he had pursued his studies in Paris as well as at Louvain – no doubt under the Gouveias at the Spanish and Portuguese Collège de Sainte-Barbe, and perhaps even as a scholar of John III.[35] If so, this would have been in the wake of the departure thence in 1533 of the pro-Erasmians André de Gouveia and his controversial successor (as

---

33. *Itinerarium Beniamini Tudelensis in quo res memorabiles, quas ante quadringentos annos totum ferè terrarum orbem notatis itineribus dimensus vel ipse vidit vel à fide dignis suæ ætatis hominibus accepit, breuiter atque dilucidè describuntur. Ex Hebraico Latinum factum Bened. Aria Montano interprete.* (Antuerpiae, ex officina Christophori Plantini, 1575). I am grateful to Dr G. Huisman of the Bibliotheek der Rijksuniversiteit Groningen for the bibliographical background to this book.

34. See Roth, *A History of the Marranos,* pp. 200, 237; Fuks-Mansfeld, 'Les Nouveaux chrétiens', p. 185.

35. H. de Vocht, *History of the Foundation and the Rise of the Collegium Trilingue Lovaniense 1517-1550,* 4 vols (Louvain, 1951-55), III (1954), 419-20; see also L. de Matos, *Les Portugais à l'Université de Paris entre 1500-1550,* Universitatis Conimbrigensis Studia ac Regesta (Coimbra, 1950), pp. 55, 88-9.

rector of the University) Nicolas Cop. It would also have been at the time when John III of Portugal, prompted partly by Juan Luís Vives, transferred the University of Lisbon to Coimbra in 1537, inviting André de Gouveia, by then rector of the Collège de Guyenne at Bordeaux, to found the College of the Arts there.[36]

Be that as it may, a vivid touch on the problems of acclimatization to the Southern Low Countries themselves is recorded by the itinerant Didacus Pyrrhus, in a letter which he wrote from Liège on his way back to Louvain on April 26, 1536, complaining to a young Portuguese friend in Antwerp, António Soares, about the bitter cold and deep snow of this horrendous Flemish spring in contrast with the warmer spring of Portugal.[37] By then, his kinsman Amatus (or rather, João Rodrigues) must have long joined him in the Southern Low Countries. Already in 1536, we find Amatus's *Index Dioscoridis* published in Antwerp by the widow of Martin Caesar; significantly, it appeared under a Latinized version of his Portuguese New Christian name 'Ioannes Rodericus Casteli Albi Lusitanus'.[38] This work's combined philological and practical medical nature even suggests a possible collaboration between the two men – one which (as I have argued elsewhere) was to continue in Italy with the publication at Venice, in 1553, of Amatus's similarly medico-philological *Enarrationes* on Dioscorides (which appeared there under his already famous Latin professional name Amatus Lusitanus). Indeed, the two friends' collaboration on Dioscorides seems even to have continued after their departure from Italy, in Dalmatian Ragusa – as is suggested by the testimony of another literary physician

---

36. On Sainte-Barbe, its Erasmian leanings under the Portuguese humanist André de Gouveia (against the inclinations of his uncle Diogo de Gouveia), the scholarships for it instituted by John III, and the transfer from Lisbon to Coimbra, see E.F. Hirsch, 'Erasmus and Portugal', *Bibliothèque d'Humanisme et Renaissance* 32 (1970), 539-57, and Matos, *Les Portugais,* pp. 125-32.

37. 'Antonio Suario Lusitano optimae spei puero S. Antuerpiam', in *F.I.E. Cato Minor* (1592), pp. 130-1; 2nd edn. (1596), pp. 86-7.

38. *Index Dioscoridis. En Candide Lector Historiales Dioscoridis campi, Exegemataque simplicium, atque eorundem Collationes cum his quae in officinis habentur, ne dum medicis, & Myropoliorum Seplasiariis, sed bonarum literarum studiosissimis perquam necessarium opus. Ioanne Roderico Casteli albi Lusitano autore.* (Excudebat Antuerpiae vidua Martini Caesaris, 1536) – every lemma being followed by the following: 'Philologia'; 'Historia Dioscoridis'; 'Iuditium Nostrum'.

and antiquarian in the following century, Sir Thomas Browne (1605-82).[39]

In Louvain, the newly-matriculated Didacus Pyrrhus wasted no time in integrating himself with Erasmus's followers there; already in March 1537 he was one of the contributors (in both Greek and Latin) to Rutger Rescius's collection of *epitaphia* for Erasmus, first published in Louvain, then re-published in Antwerp, in May to August of the same year, by the widow of Martin Caesar (who had been Amatus's printer).[40] Like the Portuguese neo-Latin poet André de Resende (1498?-1573) before him (in 1529), Didacus did not coincide in Louvain with Erasmus himself, who had long been in Switzerland, and who died there in the summer of 1536 in Basel.[41] However, in his 1547 letter from Ferrara to Giovio, Didacus does show that he had possessed a vivid secondhand acquaintance in Louvain with the great man through hearsay 'from persons most worthy of belief' about Erasmus's former favourite topics of conversations with his intimates there – in particular, the subject of the Dutch pope Hadrian VI (1522-23).[42] Moreover, Didacus further includes in the same retrospective letter to Giovio fulsome praise of his fellow townsman from Évora and predecessor at Louvain, Resende, as well as lauding the literary activity and patronage of his other compatriot, Damião de Góis (1502-74), with whom he did in fact coincide in Louvain (from 1538 onwards); he tells there with relish of de Góis's later participation in the defence of their

---

39. *In Dioscoridis Anazarbei de medica materia libros quinque Enarrationes eruditissimae doctoris Amati Lusitani medici ac philosophi celeberrimi, quibus non solum Officinarum Seplasiariis, sed bonarum etiam literarum studiosis utilitas adfertur, quum passim simplicia Graece, Latine, Italice, Hispanice, Germanice, & Gallice proponantur.* (Venetiis, apud Gualterum Scotum, 1553). On the argument for the two Portuguese scholars' continuing collaboration on Dioscorides coinciding with their joint presence in the Low Countries, Italy and Ragusa, and the corroborating testimony from Sir Thomas Browne, see Tucker, 'Didacus Pyrrhus Lusitanus', pp. 178-9.

40. Listed and described in Tucker, 'Didacus Pyrrhus Lusitanus', pp. 189-90, and reproduced in Ascenso André, 'Diogo Pires', pp. 91-7.

41. See J.C.R. Martyn (ed.), 'Life of André de Resende', in *André de Resende: On Court Life*, Bibliotheca Neolatina 3 (Bern / Frankfurt an main / New York / Paris, 1990), pp. 7-51 (p.16, and n. 12, 25-6). On Didacus, cf. also Ascenso André, 'Diogo Pires', p. 81.

42. MS Modena Est. Lat. 174, f. 161vo: 'Audivi ego de viris fide dignissimis Erasmum Rotherodammum frequenter inter suos compotores dicere solitum plura se de Hadriano pontifice, et verissime quidem posse scribere, quam olim de pseudomante Alexandro Lucianus in literas mandaverit.'

common Alma Mater against the French, in the siege of Louvain of 1542, adding that on being released by the French, de Góis subsequently returned to Portugal 'animo opinor in Indiam navigandi' ['with the intention, I think, of travelling to India'].[43] Here, Didacus's conjecture about de Gois's Indian intentions may well in fact reflect his earlier acquaintance in Louvain with de Góis's *Commentarii Rerum Gestarum in India citra Gangem a Lusitanis anno. 1538. ...*, published by Rutger Rescius in Louvain, in September 1539.[44]

Didacus may well also have been initially tutored in Latin and Greek by Joannes Varennius (van der Varen), who died in Louvain towards the end of 1536, and whose epitaph he also penned for inclusion in Rescius's *Erasmi... epitaphia* ; Varennius's *Syntaxis Linguae Graecae* had been published in Louvain a few years previously, in August 1532, by the same Rutger Rescius (in collaboration with Barthélemy Gravius).[45] Moreover, Didacus's relation with Rescius himself continued to flourish; Didacus went on to supply ample liminary verses for Rescius's Louvain edition of Euripides's *Andromache* in August 1537.[46]

Soon, his literary contributions to such academic publications by others widened in both character and scope, extending to a variety of works produced by a number of printers in Antwerp: first, liminary verse for Georgius Bontius's 1538 *Orationes Olynthicae* of Demosthenes in the Latin translation of 'Petrus Clobardus Scoundykius'; then, even more prestigiously, liminary material advertizing to the reader the merits of Gemma Phrysius's revised edition of and commentary upon Petrus Apianus's *Cosmographia,* published 'cura et impensis

---

43. MS Modena Est. Lat. 174, f. 162ro. Cf. E.F. Hirsch, 'Damião de Goes' contacts among the diplomats', *Bibliothèque d'Humanisme et Renaissance* 23 (1961), 233-51 (pp. 241-42).

44. It seems less likely, however, that in February 1547, Didacus in Italy would have derived his information from the recent publication in Portugal of *Damiani Gois Equitis Lusitani Vrbis Lovaniensis obsidio* (Olisipone, apud Lodovicum Rhotorigium, 1546).

45. Not included, however, in the later Antwerp edn.. Listed and described in Tucker, 'Didacus Pyrrhus Lusitanus', pp. 189-90. See de Vocht, *History*, I, 274 and III, 421 (and n. 2), giving October 11, as the date of death; R. Hoven, *Bibliographie de trois auteurs de grammaires grecques contemporains de Nicolas Clénard,* Livres-Idées-Société (Série in-8°), 7 (Aubel, 1985), p. 40, reproducing the epitaph, and dating the death 'au plus tard au début de 1537'.

46. Listed and described in Tucker, 'Didacus Pyrrhus Lusitanus', p. 190.

Arnoldi Berckman[n]i' in 1539 (and often reprinted); and likewise in 1539 (now on the literary side), a long eulogistic piece for Ioannes Steelsius's 'editio prima' of the *Posthomerica* of Quintus Calaber (Smyrnaeus) in the Latin translation of 'Iodocus Velaraeus', who was a personal acquaintance of Amatus Lusitanus in Antwerp;[47] then finally, in the following year 1540 (which was to be Didacus's last in the Low Countries), more liminary verse of a 'hard sell' kind, again for that cosmographical, geographical and mathematical universal genius, Gemma Phrysius (1508-55), who taught at Louvain (1532-55), and was an intimate there of Didacus's Vice-President (September 1536 – January 1539) Conrad Goclenius and of his friend Rescius (amongst others) – Didacus's liminary efforts being this time for Gemma's popular handbook the *Arithmeticae practicae methodus facilis* .[48]

Most famously of all, perhaps, Didacus seems to have been on friendly terms in the Low Countries with his fellow Iberian of *converso* – Jewish origin, the Spaniard Juan Luís Vives (b. 1492), whose death on May 6, 1540 must have followed shortly upon Didacus's own departure for Italy. Among the *Carmina* which Didacus was to publish in Ferrara, we find a poem dating from this period that mourns Vives (placing him on a par with the deceased Erasmus) whilst also praising Vives's latest, now 'orphaned', work: his pedagogic dialogues, the *Familiarum Colloquiorum Formulae, siue Linguae Latinae exercitatio...*, published in Breda, Antwerp, Basel and Cologne in 1538, re-published in 1539 (for the first of many times) in Antwerp, Basel, Paris and Lyon, and most certainly known to Didacus whilst he was still in Louvain.[49]

Now, citing the example of Vives (amongst others), Yirmiyahu Yovel, has pointed to the somewhat surprising fact that many of Erasmus's followers were Jewish *conversos* – surprising presumably because of Erasmus's notorious hostility to Judaism and Marranism, and his little truck with Christian Hebraeists such as Johannes Reuch-

---

47. See Lemos, *Amato Lusitano*, p. 76.
48. All listed and described in Tucker, 'Didacus Pyrrhus Lusitanus', pp. 190-92. On Gemma in Louvain, and his works, see de Vocht, *History*, II, 542-65.
49. 'In Ludouici Viuis colloquia' [*inc*. Belle libelle mei foetura nouissima Viuis, / E patris exequiis rapte libelle tui.], in *D.P.L. Carminum lib.* (1545), ff. G1ro-2ro. On Vives's work and its various editions, see C.G. Noreña, *Juan Luis Viues*, Archives Internationales d'Histoire des Idées 43 (The Hague, 1970), pp. 118, 302; cf. also Ascenso André, 'Diogo Pires', p. 83 (and n. 5).

lin.[50] Yet, this is perhaps to confuse the issue, at least in the case of Portuguese Marranos such as Didacus Pyrrhus, and Amatus Lusitanus, for whom, in the Imperial Low Countries, it would have been positively dangerous to show any signs of judaizing, and so of apostasy from Christianity; this would have put in doubt their *converso* status, and so invited arrest and investigation by the Inquisition. Indeed, Amatus and Didacus seem to have made a point of publicly and professionally integrating themselves indistinguishably into the academic, scholarly and medical circles of Louvain and Antwerp. Hence, for example, their very clear use of the Latinized forms of their Portuguese vernacular names in all of their publications in the Low Countries – a practice which Amatus would abandon once in Italy, but which, Didacus, by contrast, would always retain in his various poetic publications, both in Ferrara and in Ragusa, where he would merely recycle his Latinized New Christian Portuguese name '*Didacus Pyrrhus* Lusitanus' as '*Jacobus Flavius* Eborensis [of Évora]'.

Didacus's departure from the Southern Low Countries for Ferrara *circa* 1540, accompanied, or soon followed, by Amatus's, was certainly as hasty and as sudden as their departure from Lisbon had been five years previously. It seems to have been brought about not by personal choice or by the consequences of private religious indiscretion, but rather by external forces that brought a severe financial blow to the Pires family, and further dangerous exposure to the Mendes family. Didacus himself later recounted to Giovio in his 1547 letter that his family's departure for Italy had again been at his father's behest, again forcing him to interrupt his studies. The particular reason Didacus gives to Giovio is his father's 'well-considered abhorrence of the arbitrariness of legal judgments'; as a result, according to Didacus, they left for Italy, 'having left a huge fortune behind in Portugal'.[51]

Now, one of the practical, economic obstacles placed in the path of would-be New Christian emigrants by the Portuguese Kings, was the prevention of their exporting their assets abroad through the prohibition of the purchase of land or bills of exchange from them by other

---

50. Yovel, *Spinoza,* I, p. 25. On his attitude to Judaism and Christian Hebraeism, cf. Edwards, *The Jews,* pp. 50-6; cf. on the question of Erasmus's pronounced a-semitism, if not anti-semitism, see S. Markish, *Erasmus and the Jews,* transl. A. Olcott, with afterword by A.A. Cohen (Chicago, 1986).

51. MS Modena Est. Lat. 174, f. 161vo; text reproduced in Tucker, 'Didacus Pyrrhus Lusitanus', p. 183.

Portuguese subjects – a prohibition dating back to the original ban upon emigration of 1499-1507, which was subsequently renewed, as we have noted, in 1521, 1532 and 1535.[52] One of the principal ways, therefore, in which the Antwerp house of Diogo Mendes secretly helped Marranos to migrate to the Low Countries, and thence via Italy to Turkey, was to provide them with letters of credit on Antwerp in England, their first port of call, through Diogo Mendes's kinsman in the London Portuguese Marrano community, Antonio de la Roña.[53] In 1540, however, some judaizing Marrano refugees on their way to the Ottoman Empire were arrested in Milan (then directly under Spanish Imperial rule); as a result, the house of Mendes was implicated in having aided them, and the secretly Jewish Marrano community of London, which had been a key part of the Mendes's emigration network, was exposed and eventually expelled, by order of the Privy Council in February 1542, having been denounced by the Spanish Ambassador.[54] This denunciation, and the following expulsion despite the English King's earlier reassurances, are also recorded by Didacus in his letter to Giovio; significantly also, the mention of them comes just prior to Didacus's account of his family's unexpected departure for Italy and the loss of their fortune in Portugal.[55] The scandal of 1540 in Milan, and the ensuing Imperial investigation in Antwerp, must not only have made the Mendes house more vulnerable and brought dangerous suspicion upon their circle, but it must also have wrecked any chances Didacus's father may have had at that time of realizing through them the value of his Portuguese assets. It can be no coincidence either that Amatus also left Antwerp shortly afterwards to teach medicine, at

52. See Roth, *A History of the Marranos*, pp. 63, 196.
53. Roth, *A History of the Jews in England*, pp. 137-8; Roth, *A History of the Marranos*, pp. 253-4; E. Samuel, 'Le crypto-judaïsme en Angleterre, 1540-1656', in *Les Juifs d'Espagne*, pp. 147-51 (pp. 147-8).
54. See Roth, Samuel, locc. cit. in previous note above. Furthermore, Gracia Mendes herself had had legal, testimentary, problems in liquifying and transferring her late husband Francisco's assets to the younger brother's branch of the firm in Antwerp, which would also have required a royal dispensation; see H. Kellenbenz, 'I Mendes, i Rodrigues d'Evora e i Ximenes nei loro rapporti commerciali con Venezia', in *Gli Ebrei e Venezia: secoli XIV-XVIII. Atti del Convegno internazionale organizzato dall' Istituto di storia della società e dello stato veneziano della Fondazione Giorgio Cini. Venezia, Isola si San Giorgio Maggiore: 5-10 giugno 1983*, ed. G. Cozzi (Milano, 1987), pp. 143-61 (pp. 144-6).
55. MS Modena Est. Lat. 174, f. 161vo.

Ercole II's invitation, at the safe Jewish haven of ducal Ferrara (whither Didacus was also bound) – whilst Gracia Mendes, as soon as was feasible after the death of her brother-in-law Diogo Mendes (*circa* 1542-3), herself secretly liquified their assets in Antwerp with the help of her nephew João Miguez, slipping away with her household in late 1544 or early 1545, first for Venice, then for Ferrara.[56]

Ultimately, then, the story of Marrano emigration to the Southern Low Countries and beyond must be examined through its economic or mercantile aspects in conjunction with its equally undeniable religious, social and intellectual aspects. Families migrated along trade routes, and associated safe cities and ports, on a trajectory towards religious and cultural freedom, in the progressive realization of an identity. Yet often, as with the Mendes and the Pires families, some members remained behind, or tarried on the way, or even returned, sometimes acting as agents of their families' interests, and in order to do so, conforming or reverting to a Christian *converso* identity. Indeed, in the course of this study we have already noted the presence of a brother (or sister) and a nephew of Didacus back on the Iberian peninsula.

Moreover, just such an ambiguous case within what transpires to be the common family of Didacus and Amatus (who were 'blood-relatives' [*consanguinei*]) is also actually suggested by a Portuguese Inquisitorial document of 1570 on the apparent 'reconciliation' to Christianity from Judaism of one 'Abraão Cohen', also calling himself Diogo Rodrigues, after his mother's family name.[57] This twenty-two-year-old circumcised Marrano, was born and baptised in Antwerp in 1548, of Portuguese New Christian parents, and had come to Portugal to join his uncle there, one António Rodrigues de Castelo Branco, as a Christian, having first been taken, however, by his family from Antwerp to Ferrara, Ancona, and Thessalonika, where they had practised Judaism. From the rich onomastic detail and anecdotal evidence of the document, the Portuguese critic Américo da Costa Ramalho has very convincingly demonstrated that the uncle, António Rodrigues, was probably none other than a brother of Amatus Lusitanus (João Rodrigues) – a brother who had returned to Portugal from Rome.[58] Moreo-

---

56. An opinion shared by Kellenbenz, 'I Mendes', pp. 146-7; cf. also Fuks-Mansfeld, 'Les Nouveaux chrétiens', p. 187.

57. See E. Nunes, 'A Reconciliação de Abraão Cohen, 1570', *Portugaliae Historica: Revista de Historia e de Cultura Portuguesas* 2 (Lisboa, 1974), pp. 303-13.

58. Costa Ramalho, 'Didacus Pyrrhus Lusitanus', pp. 16-17.

ver, from the same documentary evidence, the young Abraão Cohen himself also emerges as a common nephew of both Didacus and Amatus; his father, Isaac Cohen, was apparently a brother of Didacus (Isaia Cohen), and his mother, Rica Rodrigues, a sister of Amatus (João Rodrigues) and António Rodrigues. It seems, therefore, that the parents Isaac and Rica remained in Antwerp professing Christianity even after the departure of their respective siblings Didacus and Amatus and the larger part of their families; they probaly remained, in fact, until the edict of Charles V expelling all New Christians from the Low Countries in 1549 – that is, the year following the birth of their son in Antwerp.[59] Even more intriguingly, the Christian vernacular name originally employed in Antwerp by the boy's father, Isaac Cohen, was not Pires, but João Mendes, no doubt after the family name of his and his brother Didacus's mother. It would transpire, therefore, that the Mendes, Pires, and Rodrigues families were by related to each other both by blood and by marriage.

Family strategies of economic survival perhaps, but also strategies pointing to the problems for the individual Marrano of finding or establishing a stable religious and cultural identity. In the particular cases of Didacus Pyrrhus and Amatus Lusitanus, neither of them would ever return to Portugal or to Imperial Antwerp, nor would they ever formerly 'reconcile' themselves to Christianity, like their nephew Abraão Cohen. Rather, in their continuing common journey beyond the Southern Low Countries – to Italy, the Dalmatian coast, and the Ottoman Empire – the poet and the physician will be seen to progress beyond an assumed Christianity, and beyond Marranism itself; yet they will do so in startlingly different, if not contradictory, ways.

C. From Marranism to Beyond? Divergent Paths, Contrasting Itineraries

In the case of Amatus, we find a steady evolution towards an open profession of Judaism in Thessalonika, fully integrating his professional and literary personae; we can see this happen in the course of his great Latin writings of medical case histories, the seven *Curationum medicinalium centuriae*, which he published principally in Paris, Lyon, Florence, Basel and Venice (1551-66).[60] Already, at the head of the

---

59. See Roth, *A History of the Marranos*, p. 238.
60. See Tucker, 'Didacus Pyrrhus Lusitanus', pp. 178-9. Most, but not all, of these first editions are listed in Lemos, *Amato Lusitano*, pp. 200-3.

fifth *Centuria* (Venetiis, ex officina Valgrisiana, 1560; Lugduni, apud Gulielmum Rovillium, 1564 & 1576), the dedicatory letter recalls the circumstances of the massacre and dispersal of the Marrano community in papal Ancona in 1556 under the anti-Jewish Theatine pope Paul IV, as well as Amatus's own consequent loss of his library there. Moreover, the letter is openly addressed from Thessalonika to one 'Josephus Nassinius Hebraeus' – that is, to no less a personage in the Ottoman Empire than the now overtly Jewish Joseph Nasi, the future Duke of Naxos, formerly João Miguez in Antwerp. Indeed, it is even dated in the Jewish fashion, 'Thessalonicae, Calend. Decemb. anno a creatione mundi 5320' [i.e. 1560].[61]

The greatest testimony, however, to Amatus's later, fully integrated, private and public espousal of Judaism is his moving physician's oath (his 'iusiurandum') of the previous year 1559, promising aid to the sick, irrespective of their wealth, creed or race; it is dated, in similar, non-Christian fashion, 'Thessalonicae datum: Anno mundi 5319' [i.e. 1559], and would have followed close upon Amatus's arrival in the Ottoman Empire *circa* 1558, after his disappointing experiences in Ragusa, where as a Jewish physician he had not been granted permission to stay and practise (probably as a result of the harsh strictures of Paul IV's infamous anti-Jewish bull of 1555, *Cum nimis absurdum*).[62] Amatus published this medical 'iusiurandum' at the end of his seventh and last *Centuria*, which recounted his medical practice in Thessalonika itself, and was published two years before his death (Venetiis, apud Vincentium Valgrisium, 1566; Lugduni, apud G. Rovillium, 1570 and 1580). The oath's very opening phrase is as much a testament to Amatus's Judaism as a guarantee of his integrity as a physician; unsurprisingly, all but the first three words mentioning 'God' were later to be expurgated in the first complete collected edition of the seven *Centuriae* in 1620.[63] The text published during the lifetime of Amatus himself, at Venice in 1566, reads:

> Iuro Deum immortalem, & sanctissima eius decem oracula, quæ liberato ab ægyptiaca seruitute populo, Mose interprete, in monte Sinar data sunt...

---

61. Cf. Tucker, 'Didacus Pyrrhus Lusitanus', p. 179.

62. For the decree of prohibition by Ragusa's Consilium Minus see Taditch, *Jevreji*, p. 277 (n. 4); cf. Tucker, 'Didacus Pyrrhus Lusitanus', p. 179.

63. *Amati Lusitani Doctoris Medici praestantissimi Curationum Medicinalium centuriae septem,...* (Burdigalae, ex Typographia Gilberti Vernoy, 1620), p. 800.

[I swear by immortal God, and his most holy ten commandments, which through the mediation of Moses were given on Mt Sinai to his people when freed from servitude in Egypt, that...][64]

Here, Amatus-Chaviv, no longer just 'Lusitanus', but also, most explicitly and confidently, an *Hebraeus*, has traversed a great spiritual as well as temporal and geographical space from the discreetly named 'Ioannes Rodericus Casteli Albi' who, fresh from Portugal, once published his *Index Dioscoridis* in Antwerp in 1536.

By contrast, the poetic figure who, from his first liminary efforts in Louvain, went on as 'Didacus Pyrrhus Lusitanus' to publish polished humanist *Carmina* (Ferrara, 1545) for the circle of Lilio Gregorio Giraldi in Ferrara and then eulogistic verse for the nobility of Ragusa – or who, later in Ragusa, as the aged 'Flavius Iacobus Eborensis', compiled his *Cato Minor* (Venice, 1592; 1596) as a pedagogic collection for the avowed edification of children and their teachers back in Counter-Reformation Lisbon – that Humanist and Catholic literary persona, is totally divorced from Didacus's *alter ego* : the private person of Isaia Cohen, whom we know from external documentation, to have been circumcised in Italy, and to have been integrated, with his father and family, in the Jewish communities of Ferrara, Ancona and Ragusa.[65]

Indeed, this divorce between the published persona – or just the public literary figure – on the one hand, and the private individual on the other, becomes even paradoxical, when we know of Didacus's informative manusucript letter of 1547 addressed from Ferrara to such an eminent literary figure as Paolo Giovio. Or again, when we read his even less guarded, much more emotive late manuscript elegies, such as the 'De exilio suo' on the circumstances of his 'exile', and the 'De Lusitanorum tumulo in Vrbe Ferraria' on the Jewish Portuguese cemetery that had been established in Ferrara in 1550; both poems were dedicated with other unpublished elegies to Domenico Slatarich (1556-

---

64. *Curationum Medicinalium Amati Lusitani medici physici praestantissimi, Centuria Septima Thessalonice curationes habitas continens, varia multiplicique doctrina referta.* (Venetiis, apud Vincentium Valgrisium, 1566), f. M1ro-2ro (f. M1ro); for discussion of other aspects of this oath, cf. Tucker, 'Didacus Pyrrhus Lusitanus', pp. 179, 188.

65. See Tucker, 'Didacus Pyrrhus Lusitanus', pp. 183-5 (and nn. 19-21, 24), and 195-99 (for the list of later Ferrarese and Ragusan works).

1607), the Ragusan rector of Padua University (from 1579).[66] These, however, are the notable exceptions.

In the very haven of ducal Ferrara itself, where the d'Estes had received Iberian Jewish refugees since 1492, and where in 1538 Ercole II had actively invited Jewish merchants to reside, granting them full rights and their own magistrature,[67] Didacus seems in fact to have kept some, if not all, of Giraldi's circle in the dark about his Judaism. It is not just that Lilio Gregorio's published *Dialogi* of 1551 omit any mention of Didacus's Marrano origins and the reasons for his cosmopolitan wanderings (an omission that might perhaps be attributed to prudent discretion); even more curiously, a letter, addressed to Didacus *circa* 1544-45 from Bartolommeo Ricci (1490-1569), reveals that this prominent Ferrarese teacher and writer of a treatise on Latin literary imitation, whom Giraldi was to make one of Didacus's interlocutors in his fictional dialogues, had little or no understanding of the circumstances of Didacus's departure from Portugal. In his letter Ricci strongly advises Didacus, somewhat inappropriately, to restore contact and ingratiate himself with his fellow scholars in Portugal by dedicating his forthcoming *Carmina* of 1545 to John III's new College of the Arts in Coimbra, lest they forget him completely, or think him dead – indeed, as if in order for him to keep open the option of a return to Portugal.[68]

This apparent ignorance or insensitivity on Ricci's part is doubly strange.[69] Firstly, because Didacus seems to have been on cordial

---

66. On these two elegies from Didacus's manuscript collection, 'Elegiarum Libri III ad Dominicum Slatarichium Patavinae Scholae Rectorem et Equitem Splendidissimum...', see C. Ascenso André (ed.), *Diogo Pires: Antologia Poética,* Textos Humanísticos Portugueses 1 (Coimbra, 1983), pp. 42-3, 84-9 (reproducing both texts); and Tucker, 'Didacus Pyrrhus Lusitanus', pp. 182-87, 197. On the establishment of the Portuguese (and Spanish) Jewish cemetery in Ferrara, see A. Pesaro, *Memorie storiche sulla communità israelitica ferrarese,* 2 vols (Ferrara 1878-80; reprinted Bologna, 1986), II (1880), 9-12.

67. See A. Balletti, *Gli Ebrei e gli Estensi* (Bologna, 1969; 1st edn. 1930), pp. 76-9.

68. On Ricci, author of *De imitatione libri tres* (Venetiis, apud Aldi filios, 1545), dedicated to Alfonso, son of Ercole II d'Este, see L. Ughi, *Dizionario storico degli uomini illustri Ferraresi,* 2 vols (Ferrara, 1804; reprinted Bologna, 1969), II, 128. L. d'Ascia, *Erasmo e l'umanesimo romano,* Biblioteca della Rivista di Storia e Letteratura Religiosa: Studi 2 (Firenze, 1991), pp. 157-9. For the text of the letter, published in Ricci's *Epistolarum libri VIII,* see Tucker, 'Didacus Pyrrhus Lusitanus', p. 181.

69. It will find a rough, literary parallel, however, in the exchange of epistolary poems appended to A. Núñez de Reinoso's 1552 pastoral allegory of exile *Clareo y Florisea* as nos. 11 and 12 of the attached *Algunas Rimas,* in which the author replies evasively to advice from a friend and fellow emigrant ('Thomas Gomez') to stop lamenting, or return to Spain; see Rose, *Alonso Núñez,* pp. 14, 89 (n. 46), 268-81.

terms with him; witness Ricci's paternal letter, and also Didacus's playful epigram 'Ad Riccium iratum' ['To an angry Riccius'], written in Ferrara and wittily alluding to Ricci's treatise *De evitanda et compescenda ira* [*On the avoidance and repression of anger*].[70] It is strange secondly, because Ricci himself was shortly to demonstrate resolute pro-Jewish sympathy by defending juridically in Ferrara Don Isaac Abrabanel, nephew of the Jewish neo-Platonist Leone Ebreo (Judah Abrabanel, *circa* 1460- after 1523) and grandson of the illustrious Biblical commentator Isaac Abrabanel (1437-1509) so deplored by Calvin; in 1546 that prominent medical scholar, courtier and member of Ferrara's Iberian Jewish community was accused by his enemies of plotting against the life of Ercole II, and was acquitted thanks to Ricci's oratorical skills of advocacy in Latin.[71]

Above all, it was the actual matter and organization of Didacus's published poetic collections that most effectively disguised his Judaism, by suggesting in fact the very opposite (and thus no doubt leading readers such as Riccius astray). For example, the principal poem opening the 1545 Ferrara *Carmina* is a celebratory epic piece of some three hundred and twenty-eight hexameter verses on the Emperor Charles V's costly campaign against Muslim Algiers in 1541.[72] Needless to say, it stands in marked contrast to Didacus's brief, disparaging mention of Charles's previous attack on Muslim Tunis of 1535-6 (which was much more successful) in his 1547 Ferrara letter to Giovio – where a 'Caesar inflated from his African triumph' is sarcastically blamed by Didacus for forcing Pope Paul III's acquiescence in establishing the

---

70. 'Niuentae id est Ferrariae. Ad Riccium iratum.' [6 eleg. distichs], in *Cato Minor* (1596), pp. 161-2.

71. On the trial, and the presence of the Abrabanel family in Ferrara, see Pesaro, *Memorie storiche*, I (1878), 22-3, II (1880), 14-15; Balletti, *Gli ebrei*, pp. 78-9. On Leone Ebreo and the elder Isaac Abrabanel, cf. C. Roth (ed.), 'Introduction', in Leone Ebreo, *The Philosophy of Love*, transl. F. Friedeberg-Seeley and J.H. Barnes (London, 1937), pp. ix-xv; C. Sirat, *A History of Jewish Philosophy in the Middle Ages* (Cambridge / Paris, 1985; 1st paperback edn. 1990), pp. 393-7, 407-10; E. Gutwirth, *Ten Centuries of Hispano-Jewish Culture: An Exhibition* (Cambridge University Library, 1992), pp. 11, 14. On Calvin's critique of Isaac Abrabanel's un-Christological commentary upon the prophecy of Daniel, see Edwards, *The Jews*, p. 61.

72. Diogo Pires, 'Caroli .V. Imperatoris ex Algeria vrbe reditus.', in *D.P.L. Carminum lib.* (1545), ff. B1vo-C4ro. On the 1541 African camaign, cf. *The New Cambridge Modern History*, Vol. II, 2nd edn.: *The Reformation 1520-1559*, ed. G.R. Elton (Cambridge, 1990), pp. 188, 390, 566, 592.

Inquisition in Portugal in 1536 (after Clement VII's previous, successful resistance).[73]

It even transpires that Didacus was not averse to using anti-semitic language himself, when it suited his rhetorical purposes. In another pro-Imperial piece, surviving in manuscript and datable to 1552, the author berates Pope Julius III as a 'half-circumcised Jew, and Indian monkey' ('Judææ semicurte, simie indice').[74] Ironically, this was in the very period when Didacus, absent from Ferrara, was tutoring Julius's great-nephew Roberto de Nobili in that other Marrano haven of papal Ancona – where, moreover, he was endeavouring to obtain through his pupil a papal safe-conduct to Rome, made necessary because of his

---

73. MS Modena Est. Lat. 174, f. 161vo: 'id quod et sanctiss. pater Paulus facturus videbatur, nisi id Caesari triumpho Aphricano inflato, ambitioseque exigenti denegare periculosum arbitraretur.'

74. Judææ semicurte, simie indice
    Hirque stolide, Infacete, qui uoraueras
    Spe, Regna, libertatem, & Vrbes Italas,
    Quid nunc struis? Quis sensus est tibi miser?
    De spe repente decidisse ten rides?
    Vides ut omnis effusus est tibi labor?
    Cum Sena restituta, desiecta omnia
    Quae nubibus suspenderas fastigia: ...
    Nectat tibi Cæsar aureum capistrum,
    Agat Tolletum, Ferdinandum´que in Crucem,
    Vos, Vos Latrones Archpiratæ impii,
    Lupi improbi: Venefici Sicarii
    Causa omnium fuistis horum Caesari
    Quae his accidere mensibus sex proximis,
    Amissio Germaniae: Turpis fuga,
    Clades nefandæ, vastitates vrbium,
    Indigna egestas, Terror undique & pauor, ...

[You semi-circumcised Jew, Indian monkey,
    Crude goat, coarse jester, who in expectation had
    Gobbled up the Realms, Liberty, and Cities of Italy,
    What now are you devising? What do you feel, you wretch?
    Do you laugh at your own short fall from expectation?
    Do you see how all your labour has been squandered?
    With the restoration of Siena, all the lofty castles
    You had built on clouds have disintegrated: ...
    May Caesar fasten you with a golden muzzle,
    May he send Toledo, and Ferdinand to the devil!
    You, you, Bandits, freebooting Pirate Captains,
    Shameless Wolves, Poisonous Assassins,
    You have been the cause of all that has befallen

own changed position in Italy as a 'circonciso', rendering him liable to trial by the Inquisition for patent apostasy from Christianity (as Roberto would point out in his obliging letter of petition on his teacher's behalf of May 1552).[75]

After the Ancona massacre of 1556, Didacus, like Amatus and many other Iberian circumcised Marranos, would move briefly to Pesaro, before passing to that further safe-haven across the Adriatic, the maritime Republic of Ragusa. Like Ferrara, Ragusa had for its own economic benefit actively welcomed Sephardic Jewish immigration since 1538, although, unlike Ferrara, it had later created a distinct Jewish

> Caesar in these last six months:
> The loss of Germany, disgraceful flight,
> Heinous disasters, cities laid to waste,
> Shameful poverty, terror and fear on all sides, ...]
> (Diogo Pires(?), *circa* 1552)

Vv. 1-8, 12-20 (of 23 vv.) of poem without title, in MS Siena, Bibl. Com. K.V.31, f. 84ro - attributable to Diogo Pires, because included amongst a group of poems by him, of which the Florentine one immediately preceding (f. 83vo), eulogizing the heir of Cosimo I de' Medici (Francesco), is datable to the same period; see Tucker, 'Didacus Pyrrhus Lusitanus', p. 195. Contrast Pires's later published poem celebrating the re-taking of Siena (from the Sienese, assisted by the French) by Spanish Imperial and Florentine forces in 1555: 'De vrbe Sena capta' [*inc.* Victa iacet Lupa nil illam iuuere Gemelli], in *F.I.E. Cato Minor* (1596), p. 162.

The piece is a curious diatribe, initially berating (apparently) the partly Sienese pope, Julius III for his fairweather support of the Emperor Charles V in Italy against the French and Ottavio Farnese, until the Imperial garrison's loss of Siena to the French in the disastrous year 1552; this year also saw the near discomfiture of Charles V, unaided either by his alienated brother Ferdinand, or by his viceroy Pedro de Toledo in Naples – who are also castigated – before the double threat of both Henri II's forces in Lorraine and of the rebellion of German princes led by the elector Maurice of Saxony, who all but took Charles prisoner at his base in Innsbruck.

On Julius's politics of prevarication in Italy, the Sienese suspicion of his support for Cosimo I's Florentine ambitions on Siena (with Imperial help), and his infamous association with a young monkey-trainer (whom he had his brother adopt, and made a cardinal), see L. von Ranke, *The History of the Popes During the Last Four Centuries,* transl. Foster, rev. G.R. Dennis, 3 vols, Bohn's Popular Library (London, 1913), I, 214-19. On Charles V's dealings in 1551-2 with Ferdinand, Pedro de Toledo and Naples, the German rebel princes and Maurice of Saxony, see Elton (ed.), *The Reformation,* pp. 192-3, 311, 371-4, 394-5.

75. See Tucker, 'Didacus Pyrrhus Lusitanus', pp. 184-5, on Roberto's letter of 20 May 1552 on Didacus's behalf.

ghetto in 1546.[76] If from 1558, Didacus would be established in Ragusa's ghetto together with his family circle, there practising as a Jew and serving as a physician, he would also practise as a poet for the Catholic Republic, obliging its ruling nobility and its literary circles.[77]

Here too, we shall find the same essential split between the public writer for a Christian literary audience and the private man of the ghetto. The compliant author of a lengthy official poem on Ragusa's patron, Saint Blasius, will not balk at including in his pedagogic *Cato Minor* at least one anti-semitic piece – a diatribe cast in hendecasyllables, in a humorous Catullan vein, from the figure of the aged poet, railing at the figure of a spendthrift Jew and parasite:[78]

In Iudæum decoctorem.

Vt omnes tibi Di, deae'que damnum
Haud vulgare duint cinæde verpe
Verpe heluo qui senis poetae
AEris millia quinque deuorasti
Vix totis (puto) quindecim diebus.
En quaenam Libya perusta monstrum
Hoc nobis dedit? heus sceleste verpe
Parcum, & fruge bona virum putauit
Harpya inuenio rapaciorem.

[Against a spendthrift Jew.

May all the Gods and goddesses inflict upon you
No ordinary harm, you circumcised sodomist,
You circumcised glutton, who have an aged poet's
Five thousand asses devoured
In scarcely fifteen days (I think) all told.
Why, what scorched Libya has given
This monster to us? eh? you circumcised scoundrel!
Thrifty and frugal he thought the man;
I find him more rapacious than a harpy.]
(Diogo Pires, *Cato Minor* (1596 [only]))[79]

---

76. See B. Krekić, 'Gli ebrei a Ragusa nel Cinquecento', in Cozzi (ed.), *Gli Ebrei*, pp. 835-44 (pp. 839-40); Israel, *European Jewry*, p. 34.

77. See Tucker, 'Didacus Pyrrhus Lusitanus', pp. 183-4.

78. On Didacus's manuscript poem 'De divo Blasio, rhacusanae reipublicae patrono' [circa 400 hexameter verses], see Tucker, 'Didacus Pyrrhus Lusitanus', p. 198.

79. *F.I.E. Cato Minor* (1596), pp. 177-8; poem not included in earlier 1592 edn.. Cf. Catullus, *Carmina*, 25 and 47.

Moreover, the whole collection of the *Cato Minor*, dedicated to the schoolteachers of Lisbon, will in both its editions of 1592 and 1596, be solemnly prefaced by a guarantee of conformity to the teachings of the Church, personally addressed to the author by none other than the Carmelite Inquisitor General of Louvain himself.[80]

In many ways this is a symbolic return – back to Louvain, back to the Portugal of the Inquisition, and, more poignantly, back to that well-meant advice given in Ferrara by the kindly Bartolommeo Ricci: that the itinerant poet should not allow himself to be forgotten by his compatriots back home. Yet, this is also but one half of Didacus Pyrrhus's own particular way of moving, like Amatus Lusitanus, beyond Marranism: that is, beyond the confused oscillation between Catholic and Jew that has been documented by Brian Pullan, and beyond that inner 'exile within exile' – from an essential Jewish self as well as from external Catholic society – that has been adumbrated by Yirmiyahu Yovel.[81] Didacus Pyrrhus-Iacobus Flavius's artistic, literary self stands separate from his other, hidden, barely expressed, Jewish self, privately lived in Ferrara and in the ghetto of Ragusa, and no doubt secretly lived before then in Louvain and Antwerp. These two divided selves stand apart also, however, from the fully integrated person and persona of the scholarly physician Amatus Lusitanus, whose own, very different itinerary beyond Antwerp, Ferrara and Ragusa, and beyond Marranism, towards an open assumption of Jewish identity, at once existential and literary, in Ottoman Thessalonika, could not properly be acknowledged by 'Flavius Jacobus Eborensis' – that poet of Ragusa who penned and published Amatus's epitaph, certainly, but who made no allusion in it to the crucial, open fact of his friend's Judaism. The fulfilment of that particular duty of sympathy and brotherhood, would no doubt have been reserved for the other half of Diogo Pires – the shadowy, private figure called Isaia Cohen, that discreet inhabitant of Ferrara and of the ghetto of Ragusa, and that once secretive student of Louvain, whom we shall never properly know.

---

80. See 'F. Eusebius Carmelita haeretice prauitatis Inquisitor Generalis apud Louanienses Flaui Iacobo. S.D.', and 'Flauius Iacobus Eborensis Olyssipponensibus, Ludimagistris. S.D. ... D, Rhacusae. Idib. sext. ann. V. MDXCII.' (as well as title-page), in F.I.E. *Cato Minor* (1592), ff. A2ro-vo, A3ro-4ro; (1596), ff. A2ro-vo, A3ro-vo.

81. Pullan, *The Jews of Europe*, pp. 211-28; Yovel, *Spinoza*, I, 22-4.

INDEX

Abendino, Çag : 6
Abenpesat, Vidal: 10
Abrabanel, Isaac: 12, 13, 17, 109
Abrabanel, Judah (Leo Ebraeus): 109
Abraham b. Hya: 8
Abraham b. Eleazar Ha-Levi, ibn Shraga: 12
Abulafia, Abraham: 7
Agricola, Rodolphus: 71
Ahasverus: 10
Alamany, Juan: 15, 18-22
Alcalá de Henares: 64, 78, 79
Alexander IV, pope: 24
Alfonso d'Este: 109
Amatus Lusitanus: vide Rodrigues de Castelo Branco, João:
Amsterdam: 87
Anchieta, Juan: 17
Ancona: 88, 93, 104, 106, 108, 110, 111
Antwerp: 87-90, 94-105, 113
Apianus, Petrus: 100
Aragón, Pedro de: 11
Aragonés, Isaac: 12
Aragonés, Za: 11
Arias, Ysabel: 10
Augustine: 24, 26, 30, 31, 32, 35, 60, 72-74
Avila, Antonio de: 10-12
Ayala, Lopez de: 43
Azamar, Pedro: 22

Báñez, Domingo: 54
Barba, Juan: 17-19, 22
Barcelona: 12, 18, 23, 25, 26, 28, 46
Benardut, Jehuda: 8
Benedict XIII, pope: 28
Benjamin of Tudela: 96
Berckmannus, Arnoldus: 101
Bernáldez, A.: 49
Blanche of Castile: 28
Boniface VIII, pope: 53
Bontius, Georgius: 100
Breda: 71
Browne, Thomas: 99
Bruges: 69, 70

Caesar, Martin: 99
Calatayud: 8, 10

Carbonell, Johan: 18, 22
Cardoso, Fernando (Jitzhaq Cardoso): 89
Castro, Américo: 37
Cervantes, Miguel de: 1, 2
Charles V, emperor: 43, 60, 71, 86, 91, 97, 105, 109
Chiquitilla (Giqatilia), Joseph: 15
Christiani, Pablo: 26
Cisnéros, Ximenez de: 43
Clement IV, pope: 24
Clement VII, pope: 84-86, 91, 110
Clobardus Scoundykius, Petrus: 100
Cohen, Abraão: 104, 105
Cohen, Isaac Ha-: 15
Cohen, Isaac: 105
Cohen, Isaia: vide Pires, Diogo
Coimbra: 98
Colón, Hernando: 22
Columa, Pietro (Petrus Galatinus): 11
Columbus, Christopher: 19, 22
Constantinople: 13, 93, 97
Cop, Nicolas: 98
Coronel, Louis: 75
Cota, Ruy (Rodrigo): 1
Craneveldius, Franciscus: 68, 69
Croÿ, Charles of : 64
Cubero, Yento (Shem Tov): 2, 3, 9, 10

Dagdayiron: 19
David ben Jospeh Abudarham: 3
de los Ríos, Amadar: 36
Del regimiento de príncepes: 53
Diez de Games, A.: 19
Dixer, Miquel: 69
Dominic, saint: 29
Donin, Nicholas: 24, 25

Ebraeus, Leo: vide Abrabanel, Judah
Eiximenis, Francesch: 11, 22
Encina, Juan de: 1, 2
Erasmus, Desiderius: 43, 64, 68, 69, 71, 72, 78, 79, 99, 102
Ercole II of Ferrara: 104, 108, 109
Espina, Alonso de: 31
Espinosa, Diego de: 48
Esplugas, Gracia de: 9
Eymeric, Nicholas: 52

Ferdinand III of Aragón: 20-22, 50
Fernandez, Antonio: 97
Ferrara: 88, 89, 93-96, 99, 102, 104, 107-109, 111, 113
Ferrari, Giolito de': 95
Ferrer, Sibila: 65
Ferrer, Vicent: 23, 29, 30, 46
Fevynus, Johannes: 69
Flavius Eborensis: vide Pires, Diogo

Games, Diéz de: 19, 21
García, Antonio: 40
Gemma Frisius: 100, 101
Geronimo de Santa Fé (Joshua Halorki): 27
Giovio, Paolo (sive Jovius): 94, 97, 99, 102, 103, 107, 109
Giqatilia (Chiquitilla), Joseph: 16
Giraldi, Lilio Gregorio: 94, 107, 108
Goclenis, Conrad: 101
Góis, Damião de: 99, 100
Gonçalez de la Oz, Gómez: 10
Gouveia, André de: 97, 98
Gouveia, Diogo de: 98
Granada: 17
Granada, Talavera de: 56, 60
Gravius, Barthélemy: 100
Gregory IX, pope: 23, 25

Hadrian VI, pope: 85, 99
Halorki, Joshua (Geronimo de Santa Fé): 27
Henry VIII of England: 64, 69, 70, 94
Innocent IV, pope: 24

Isidorus (Pseudo-): 17, 22

James of Aragón: 28
Jerusalem: 3, 13, 17
Joachim of Fiore: 11, 12, 19
John III of Portugal: 86, 87, 90, 97, 98, 108
John XXII, pope: 24
Joseph ibn Shraga: 17, 19
Joshua, son of Levy: 6
Juan el Viejo: 5-8
Julius III, pope: 86, 110

Landi, Ortensio: 95
Las Casas, Bartolomé de: 22
Leo X, pope: 84-86

Libro del Alborayque: 20
Liège: 98
Lisbon: 21, 93, 98, 113
Llorente, Pint: 39, 40
London: 69, 94, 103
Louvain: 78, 80, 88-91, 95, 98-101, 103, 113
Lull, Ramon: 29
Luna, Beatrix de: vide Mendez, Gracia

Maimonides: 14, 23, 25
Manrique, Alonso: 38, 75
Manrique, Diego: 77
Manuel I of Portugal: 85-96
Manutius, Paulus: 84
March, Blanca: 65-68, 70
Marcuello, Pedro de: 16, 22
Martín Población, Juan: 75
Martínez de Ampiés, Martín: 15
Martini, Raymund: 25
Medici, Giovanni de' (Leo X): 84-86
Medici, Giulio de'(Clement VII): 84-86, 91, 110
Medici, Lorenzo de': 84
Melamed, Jacob: 10 ?
Mendes, Diogo: 95, 96, 103, 104
Mendes, Gracia (Beatrix de Luna, Gracia Nasi) : 94-96, 103, 104
Menéndez Pelayo, Marcelino: 35
Merlin: 19
Methodius (Pseudo-): 14
Miguez, João (Joseph Nasi, Josephus Nassinus Hebraeus): 95, 104, 106
Milan: 103
Molcho, Salomon (Diogo Pires): 86
Montoro, Antón de: 1, 2
Montpellier: 25

Núñez de Reinozo, Alonso: 95, 96, 108
Núñez, Fernando: 91
Nasi, Gracia: vide Mendez, Gracia
Nasi, Joseph: vide Miguez, João
Nassinus Hebraeus, Josephus (Joseph Nasi, João Miguez): vide Miguez, João
Nebrija, Antonio de: 68, 79
Netanyahu, B.: 39, 40
Niño, Pero: 19
Nobili, Roberto de: 110, 111
Nutius, Martinus: 95

Oxford: 69

Palencia, Alonso de: 20
Paris: 23, 25, 26, 28, 78-80, 97
Paul III, pope: 58, 86, 91, 109
Paul IV, pope: 106
Peratallada: 11
Pesaro: 111
Peter the Venerable: 25
Petrus Alcyonus: 83-89
Petrus Alfonsi: 25, 71
Petrus Galatinus (Pietro Columna): 11
Pires, Diogo (Didacus Pyrrhus Lusitanus, Isaia Cohen, Flavius Eborensis): 44, 83, 88-113
Pires, Diogo (Salomon Molcho): 86
Publilius Syrus: 73
Pulgar, Hernando del: 22
Pyrrhus Lusitanus, Didacus: vide Pires, Diogo

Ragusa: 88, 89, 93, 98, 102, 106, 107, 110, 112
Ramírez de Lucena, Juan: 9
Ramírez de Villaescusa, Diego: 2
Rashi: 24
Raymond of Peñafort: 25, 26
Rescius, Rutger: 99-101
Resende, André de: 99
Reuchlin, Johann: 101
Révah, I.S.: 39, 41, 42
Ribeiro, Bernardim: 95, 96
Riber, Lorenzo: 37
Ricci, Bartolommeo: 108, 109, 113
Rivkín, E.: 40
Roña, Antonio de la: 103
Rocatallada, Joan de: vide Roquetaille, Jean de
Rodericus Casteli Albi, Joannes: 107
Rodrigues de Castelo Branco, António: 104
Rodrigues de Castelo Branco, João: 44, 83, 88-113
Rodrigues, Diogo: 104
Rodrigues, Rica: 105
Roquetaillade, Jean de: 11-13, 15
Rossi, Arariah dei: 13
Rovillius, Gulielmus: 106
Rozas Ysla, Juan de : 10

Salamanca: 78, 91-93

Santangel, Antón de: 8, 9
Segovia: 10-13, 46
Sepher Ha-Meshiv: 18
Sevilla: 20, 21, 46, 54
Shem Tov ben Joseph ben Shem Tov (Yento Cubero): 2, 3, 9, 10
Sixt IV, pope: 57
Slatarich, Domenico: 107
Soares, António: 98
Solomon b. Samuel Ha-Sefardi: 22
Soria: 10
Soto, Dominico de: 91
Spinoza, Baruch: 89
Summula seu Breviloquium super concordia Novi et Vetuseris Testamentis: 11
Steelsius, Johannes: 101

Talavera, Hernando de: 48
Thessaloniki: 88, 93, 104-106, 113
Toldot Adam: 7
Torquemada, Juan de: 50, 53
Tortosa: 23-29
Trovas of Bandarra: 11
Turmeda, Anselm: 15

Usque, Samuel: 95, 96

Valencia: 13, 46, 69, 70, 78, 80
Valgrisius, Vincentius: 106
Valla, Lorenzo: 71
Valladolid: 80
Valldaura, Margarita: 69
Valldaura, Nicolás: 52
Varennius (Van der Varen), Joannes: 100
Vassaeus, Didacus: 89
Velaraeus, Iodocus: 101
Venice: 89, 98, 104, 106
Vergara, Juan de: 59, 62, 64, 71, 77, 78
Vergilius Maro, Publius: 90, 96
Vieira, António: 11
Villanova, Arnoldo de: 11, 12, 15
Virriés, Alonso: 62
Vives, Joan Luís: 35-81, 98, 101

Yanin: 19
Yehiel of Paris: 25

Zacuto, Abraham: 12, 17
Zaragoza: 9

PRINTED ON PERMANENT PAPER • IMPRIME SUR PAPIER PERMANENT • GEDRUKT OP DUURZAAM PAPIER - ISO 9706

ORIENTALISTE, KLEIN DALENSTRAAT 42, B-3020 HERENT